Christian Madsbjerg is a founder of ReD Associates and the Director of its New York office. ReD is a strategy consulting company based

anthropologists, soc

Christian studied

Copenhagen and London. He lives in New York City.

Sensemaking

*What Makes Human Intelligence Essential
in the Age of the Algorithm*

———— ✺ ————

CHRISTIAN MADSBJERG

Little, Brown

LITTLE, BROWN

First published in the US in 2017 by Hachette Books, a division of Hachette Book Group, Inc.
First published in Great Britain in 2017 by Little, Brown

13 5 7 9 10 8 6 4 2

A CIP catalogue record for this book
is available from the British Library.

Hardback ISBN: 978-1-4087-0836-1
C-format ISBN: 978-1-4087-0837-8

Printed and bound in Great Britain by
Clays Ltd, St Ives plc

Papers used by Little, Brown are from well-managed forests
and other responsible sources.

Little, Brown
An imprint of
Little, Brown Book Group
Carmelite House
50 Victoria Embankment
London EC4Y 0DZ

An Hachette UK Company
www.hachette.co.uk

www.littlebrown.co.uk

Contents

Foreword

The End of Thinking

1.

A senior executive at one of the world's largest health care technology companies sits in a conference room filled with whiteboards. PowerPoint slides blink by on a projector screen. After growing in the double digits for almost a decade and securing a comfortable lead in the market for diabetes care products, the EVP's department has missed its sales targets for the third time this year. A few months ago, he signed off on an extensive round of market research to understand why. The marketers conducted surveys with thousands of diabetes patients all over the United States and Europe, measuring hundreds of different factors that account for their compliance in taking their medication. He learned that "43 percent of Type 2 diabetes patients are noncompliant, and 84 percent of those noncompliant patients cite forgetfulness as the main reason for their noncompliance." With only a short period of time to turn the company around before the board tears into him, the EVP is consumed with anger. "We already know that patients are noncompliant because they forget. We've known that for decades. We need to know what we can do to get them to change their behavior." The room is silent. After millions of dollars and months of research, no one in the room has any idea why people do what they do.

2.

A candidate for Senate in a battleground state reviews the polling averages for her race. Her consultants tell her that the averages, when properly adjusted to reflect the current environment, assure her a win in November. They have sliced her electorate into ever-narrowing segments so she can shape her talking points accordingly. We've seen this before, *they say.* This November will be like the last election and the one before. *But over the spring, something completely unexpected happens. A surprising new candidate puts his hat in the ring. Instead of talking points and segmentation, he captures the imagination of the electorate with an oratorical gift, weaving together seemingly disparate cultural themes and patterns into a powerful metaphor for the future. When the frontrunner watches a video of one of his rallies, she can see the swell of energy and excitement in the voters. The mood of the event fills her with a deep sense of foreboding. With all the numbers showing support for her campaign, why does it feel as though this man is making a more meaningful connection with the voters than she? In a moment of terror, it dawns on her that she is going to lose this election despite doing everything exactly right.*

3.

An entrepreneur at a start-up specializing in solar power solutions struggles to make sense of changes in the market. As energy distribution moves from a centralized model—provided by utilities

*over the grid—to an increasingly distributed model with a con-
stellation of players, the entrepreneur must synthesize a variety of
different data streams. Her team prides itself on its engineering
expertise—cutting-edge technical knowledge of the solar market—
so they spend little time dealing with all of the cultural and political dynamics that occur within corporate sustainability initiatives.
And yet, despite their industry knowledge, her company is losing
clients. Just today, one of their biggest corporate clients, a retail
chain eager to use sustainability initiatives in their marketing
platforms, announced that they were signing on with another solar
company selling products technically inferior and more expensive
than the product she is offering. She must find partners to replace
them immediately or she won't make company payroll in a month
or two.* Why are we losing market share to competitors with far
less technical knowledge? *she thinks.* What are we missing?

⌒⌣⌒

Although the word *algorithm* is in the subtitle, this is not really
a book about algorithms. Nor is this a book about computer
programming or the future of machine learning. This is a book
about people. More specifically, this is a book about culture
and the pendulum shifts of our age. Today we are so focused
on STEM-based knowledge—theories from science, technology, engineering and math, and the abstractions of "big
data"—that alternative frameworks for explaining reality have
been rendered close to obsolete. This pendulum shift is doing
great damage to our businesses, governments, and institutions.
As each of these three scenarios illustrates, society devalues our
human inferences and judgments at a great cost. Our fixation
with STEM erodes our sensitivity to the nonlinear shifts that

occur in all human behavior and dulls our natural ability to extract meaning from qualitative information. We stop seeing numbers and models as a representation of the world and we start seeing them as the truth—the *only* truth. We are in grave danger of completely eroding our sense of the human world in favor of these false abstractions.

Of course, the hard sciences are a good way of explaining quite a lot on our planet, namely material nature. They are tremendously effective at explaining chemistry, engineering, or physics, for example. *But they are not good at explaining us.* As the famed physicist Neil deGrasse Tyson put it, "In science, when human behavior enters the equation, things go nonlinear. That's why physics is easy and sociology is hard."

Because, at the end of the day, it doesn't matter how much hard data we have in our hands, how many brain scans we've monitored on our screens, or how many different ways we have segmented our markets. If we don't have a perspective on the human behavior involved, our insights have no power. When we lose touch with the human circumstances present inside every single election, behind every breakout innovation and each and every successful corporate initiative, we limit our ability to genuinely understand our world.

If we want to truly make sense of our challenges, we must return to a process that feels old-fashioned and out of date in today's anesthetizing world of algorithmic promise. It's something that has been sorely lacking in all of our organizations and across all aspects of our civic discourse. It's called critical thinking. And, as a process, it has never felt so revolutionary nor so cutting edge.

Introduction

The Human Factor

The essence of being human is that one does not seek perfection.

—*George Orwell*, In Front of Your Nose: 1945–1950

We humans have been getting some bad press lately. Not a day goes by without hearing about how irrational or inefficient we are when compared with machines. Next to our sleek silicon-powered computer counterparts, our brains are sluggish and burdened by emotions. In the work world, humans are basket cases, slowing down projects and turning black and white lines into gray with our penchant for ambiguity and complexity. We need to learn through experience, and what we learn doesn't have the same precision, rigor, or consistency as algorithms.

Our standing in the world has fallen so far that we have developed a mantra to excuse ourselves from our inadequacies. "I'm only human," we shrug to coworkers in the break room or at happy hour drinks. This idiom contains a singular truth about the way our culture conceives of our humanity: to be human is to be full of flaws.

In engineering circles, this is referred to as the human factor.

The human factor—in domains as varied as aeronautics, supply chain management, and pharmaceuticals—is another way of saying: the capacity for error. There is even a burgeoning area of scholarship called human factors research, focused on how to optimize and correct for our flaws in human-computer interaction, or HCI. Human factors research explores how machines can best cope when we humans make one of our typical mistakes. Google utilizes human factors research, for example, when one of their driverless cars attempts to interpret the inconsistencies of a real human driver. Humans are notorious for behaving irregularly, frustrating the efforts of algorithms to achieve driving perfection.

To add to our list of woes, journalists and futurists are telling us that we humans will soon be turning over the majority of our jobs to robots. Factory and customer service employees have been the first to go, but it will soon be entire swaths of our labor force: restaurant workers, pharmacists, medical diagnosticians, lawyers, accountants—even caretakers for the elderly. For journalists and academics, the question is not *if* this will happen, but rather what we will do with ourselves *when* it happens.

The solution to the human problem seems straightforward. If we want to remain useful—and employed—we should cede territory to the algorithms all around us—even become subservient to them. Not a day goes by without hearing about a new *Moneyball* fix—bringing an Ivy League–educated economist in to crack open an industry with clean, fact-based analysis rather than human intuition and experience. We are inundated with stories of big data scores from Amazon, Google, and countless other apps and start-ups. Employment website Glassdoor named "data scientist" as the number-one job in America for 2016 based on the number of job openings, salary, and advancement opportunities. We fervently believe that more data will lead to more insights. If we learn X from looking at a data set of one hundred people, wouldn't we learn exponentially more after aggregating a data set of hundreds of thousands of people? Or hundreds of millions? Or billions? Facebook CEO Mark Zuckerberg captured our intoxication with big data when he recently told investors that he wanted machine learning at Facebook to create "the clearest model of everything there is to know in the world."

Our students are getting the message. At the most prestigious universities in the United States, liberal arts fields like English and history used to be among the most popular majors, but a surge in interest in engineering and the natural sciences has decimated many humanities departments. Since the 1960s, the number of degrees awarded in the humanities has shrunk by half. Funding for humanities research has declined precipitously. In 2011, it amounted to less than half of a percent of the funds for science and engineering research and development. Within the social sciences, quantitative studies like social network analysis and psychometrics dominate, while qualitative fields like sociology and anthropology are seen as passé. At a 2015 town hall meeting, U.S. Republican presidential candidate Jeb Bush told the audience that students majoring in disciplines like psychology were headed for jobs at Chick-fil-A. That same year, the Japanese education minister ordered Japanese universities to shut down social science and humanities departments or convert them "to serve areas that better meet society's needs."

The humanities—disciplines that explore culture, such as literature, history, philosophy, art, psychology, and anthropology—no longer meet "society's needs." A humanities-based understanding of different people and their worlds is now officially useless. After all, compared to the endless information accessible through big data, what value is there in human-led cultural inquiry? What value is there in actually reading a few great books when algorithms can "read" them all and give us an objective analysis of their content? What value is there in plays, paintings, historical studies, dances, political treatises, and pottery, in cultural knowledge that cannot be stripped of its specificity and context and transformed into vast sluices of information?

I write this book with one urgent message to impart: *there most certainly is value.*

We dismiss this cultural knowledge—cultivated through humanities thinking—at great risk to our future. When we focus solely on hard data and natural science methods—when we attempt to quantify human behavior only as so many quarks or widgets—we erode our sensitivity to all the forms of knowledge that are not reductionist. We lose touch with the books, music, art, and culture that allow us to experience ourselves in a complex social context.

This is not an esoteric subject for debate solely inside the ivory tower. In fact, I see the consequences of this phenomenon playing out in my consulting work every day. I see the dearth of cultured leadership at the senior levels of major corporations. Too many of the top cadre of leadership I have met are isolated in their worldview. They have lost touch with the humanity of their customers and their constituents and, as a result, they mistake numerical representations and models for real life. Their days are sliced and diced into tiny segments, so they feel they don't have time to wander around in the mess of real-world data. Instead, they jump into a problem-solving process and a conclusion without understanding the actual question.

As a result of all this, they tend to hire engineering- or MBA-trained junior executives to be their foot soldiers in the data trenches. Their fixation with hard data often masks stunning deficiencies, and many such lower-level managers will hit a glass ceiling in today's business world. They are reductionists without the sensitivity to recognize the most exciting and essential patterns. These are managers who did everything "right": they hacked the system and aced all the tests; they went to the best schools and got all the good grades; they spent their entire education training their minds to reduce the problems and then to solve them. And today, as a result, they simply don't have the intellectual sophistication required to move into the upper echelons of leadership.

It's not always easy to prove this point—that training in the humanities and the social sciences is just as important, if not *more* important, than STEM to a successful career—with hard data. But allow me to put this data question in context. In 2008, the *Wall Street Journal* reported on a large-scale study of global compensation by the research firm PayScale Inc. The study confirms that students with a pure STEM background generally get better-paying jobs right after graduating from college. Massachusetts Institute of Technology (MIT) and California Institute of Technology rank as the top two schools for starting *median* salary—at $72,000—and then at number 3 and 6, respectively, for the best mid-career *median* salaries.

But this study includes everyone who graduated from college

across the whole of the United States, so *median* measurements both for starting salaries and for mid-career salaries favor STEM graduates. This is because the liberal arts graduates end up working in an incredibly wide range of jobs and fields across the whole of the nation. If you look at the most successful earners in the entire country—in the 90th percentile mid-career and beyond—the story starts to change. MIT doesn't show up until number 11, behind ten colleges and universities with strong liberal arts concepts. Places like Yale University and Dartmouth College show the strongest median earnings—above $300,000. Of all other engineering STEM-centered colleges, only Carnegie Mellon University even makes the list of mid-career 90th percentile salaries.

The study reveals the same story about majors. Generally, computer engineering and chemical engineering are high-ranking majors when it comes to salary, while it is much harder to find the humanities on the top 20 majors list when it comes to higher earners mid-career. But, again, if you look at the *most successful* 90th percentile earners in the whole of the country, suddenly political science, philosophy, drama, and history are placed prominently, often from pure liberal arts schools like Colgate University, Bucknell University, and Union College.

What we can take away from this data is that most STEM training will get students a good income at the starting gate and a decent career. But powerful earners—the people running the show, breaking through the glass ceilings, and changing the world—tend to have liberal arts degrees. This will come as surprising news if you listen to the general rhetoric coming out of Silicon Valley, politicians, and even amongst many leaders in education today. But, if you have spent any time in a global company or one of the world's most powerful institutions, it makes sense. After nearly twenty years of counseling the very top executives and management around the world, I can tell you that the most successful leaders are curious, broadly educated people who can read both a novel and a spreadsheet.

After all, do we actually think that figuring out the future of a global insurance company or discerning the political and social implications of proposed legislation is a process based entirely on a linear decision tree or a set of numbers on a spreadsheet? In February 2007, Lehman Brothers had all of its balance sheets in order and reported a record high market cap of close to $60 billion. Little more than a year later, their stock had plunged 93 percent and they were filing for bankruptcy. Numerical data sets obscured the more complex reality that led to the Lehman Brothers collapse. In 2003 and 2004, the bank had acquired five mortgage lenders, including two sub-prime mortgage lenders that loaned money to borrowers without any real documentation. In the midst of a housing boom, the profits were unprecedented, but more and more people were gaining access to free money with less and less scrutiny of their ability to repay any of it. Meanwhile, these bad loans were being hidden away with all of the more legitimate loans, packaged together in complex financial products called CDOs, or collateralized debt obligations. The reality on the streets was available to any leader or executive willing to go out and observe it. It was inevitable that most of the borrowers in the sub-prime mortgage market were going to default. Unfortunately for all of us who had retirement savings invested in the stock markets in September 2008, few financial leaders found it worth their time to take their cues from real-world data. When we stop thinking, it's not just our intellects that are at stake. It's our businesses, our educations, our governments, and our life savings.

I am not alone in my concern. Many of our most prominent leaders are publicly calling out for more liberal arts–trained thinkers to meet this coming future. Norman Augustine, retired chairman and CEO of Lockheed Martin, wrote an op-ed for the *Wall Street Journal* in 2011 arguing for a stronger foundation in the humanities in our primary and secondary schools: "Far more than simply conveying the story of a country or civilization, an education in history can create critical thinkers who can digest, analyze, and synthesize information and articulate their findings. These are skills needed across a broad range of subjects and disciplines."

A. G. Lafley, former CEO of Procter & Gamble, had one single piece of advice for achieving business success in today's complex managerial environment: pursue a degree in the liberal arts. "By studying art, science, the humanities, social science, and languages," he wrote in the *Huffington Post*, "the mind develops the mental dexterity that opens a person to new ideas, which is the currency for success in a constantly changing environment. And just as an aspiring Major League pitcher needs a live arm and a calculating, cool head to pitch effectively, so too does a management prospect need to be educated broadly to respond effectively to ambiguity and uncertainty. Completing a broad liberal arts curriculum should enable a student to develop the conceptual, creative, and critical thinking skills that are the essential elements of a well-exercised mind."

These leaders, like so many others at the forefront of business, policy, and entrepreneurship, are sounding the alarm for a better-educated workforce. After all, it was not so long ago when it was commonplace for leaders in finance, media, or policy to have a background in the humanities: Ken Chenault, current CEO of American Express, cited his in-depth study of history as a touchstone for his leadership and managerial acumen; Sam Palmisano, former CEO of IBM, was a history major at Johns Hopkins; Hank Paulson, once secretary of the Treasury, studied English at Dartmouth; Carly Fiorina, CEO of Hewlett Packard from 1999 to 2005, described her undergraduate major in medieval history as the perfect foundation for understanding the high-tech world; Michael Eisner of Disney bypassed business and finance courses, eschewing them for majors in English and theater; famed investor Carl Icahn's senior thesis in philosophy at Princeton was titled, "The Problem of Formulating an Adequate Explication of the Empiricist Criterion of Meaning"; Sheila Bair, former FDIC chair, studied philosophy as an undergraduate at the University of Kansas; and Stephen Schwarzman, chairman and CEO of the private equity firm Blackstone, chose an interdisciplinary major at Yale that he described as "psychology, sociology, anthropology, and biology, which is really sort of the study of the human being."

More and more people, however, have come to view these disciplines as irrelevant when compared with the immediate utility of a degree in data analytics or an online crash course in the latest computer programming skill. The result of this cultural shift is that we stop seeing value in things like poetry, sculpture, novels, and music. And when we devalue humanistic endeavors, we lose our best opportunity for exploring worlds different from our own. When I read a great novel like Thomas Mann's *The Magic Mountain*, I can actually feel the devastation of a European continent during and after World War I; when I encounter a medieval tapestry like *The Hunt of the Unicorn*, I understand what was meaningful to people in France on the cusp of the Renaissance. And when I visit the Ryōan-ji Zen garden in Kyoto, the placement and texture of the stones shows me something essential about the Japanese worldview and aesthetic.

Whether you are studying Chinese architecture, Mexican history, or the philosophy of the Sufis, this kind of thinking trains our minds to synthesize all types of data, to explore without need of proving or disproving a narrow hypothesis, and to engage empathically with the particularities of a given world. I believe that this type of cultural engagement is an essential training ground for understanding *any* group of people. If you work for a pharmaceutical firm, for example, you need to understand the world of a person with diabetes, or all your attempts at drug development will surely fail. Say you make cars. You need to know what life is like for a driver living in western China, or your vehicles will be filled with irrelevant features in the world's largest car market. And if you work in the public sector, you need social science tools to think critically about the culture of bureaucracy.

Experiences with the humanities teach us how to imagine other worlds. But they offer so much more than that. Because when we can fully imagine other worlds—using cultural knowledge and explanations for our human experience—we inevitably develop a more acute perspective on our own world. We learn to see when models and financial innovations are diverging from the truth. We recognize patterns—distilled from both scientific facts and practical reality, from both existing situations and future possibilities—that shed light on insights and, ultimately, help us form a genuine perspective. And perspectives, in the long run, always prove far more profitable—to both your bank account and your life—than confinement in a cage of data.

This rigorous cultural engagement is the foundation of the practice I call *sensemaking*. Academics have used the term *sensemaking* to describe different concepts over the years, but I use it here, throughout this book, simply to describe an ancient practice of cultural inquiry, a process based on a set of values we are in great danger of forgetting. With sensemaking, we use human intelligence to develop a sensitivity toward meaningful differences—what matters to other people as well as to ourselves.

In the pages to come, sensemaking will take us on an intellectual adventure story grounded in the tenets of twentieth-century philosophy. We will look at the theories and methodologies that make up studies in the humanities and discuss different ways that these can help us extract meaning from nonlinear data. We will examine our genuine experience of creative insights and, in so doing, clear away some of the misguided notions that continue to circulate around innovation and breakout ideas. And we will meet master practitioners and look at how human intelligence is the only intelligence that can cultivate a perspective.

Never before has our culture been so seduced by the promises of artificial intelligence, machine learning, and cognitive computing. Never before has our world of overlapping political, financial, social, technical, and environmental systems been so inextricably linked. We must remind ourselves—and the culture at large—why the human factor is the most important factor when it comes to making sense of this world. The time to begin is right now.

Chapter One

Making Sense of the World

True genius resides in the capacity for evaluation of uncertain, hazardous, and conflicting information.

—*Winston Churchill*

The first thing a visitor to the headquarters of the Ford Motor Company will notice upon arrival is the flags. They surround the entrance to the imposing blue building in Dearborn, Michigan, each one from a country where Ford has operations. There are so many flags that the long walkway up to the main door of the building has the air of a United Nations assembly.

The lobby and lower floors of the headquarters maintain this atmosphere of diplomatic cheerfulness—people come and go with a friendly efficiency, dinging the countless elevators doing brisk business up and down. The very top floors of the headquarters, however, are oddly quiet. This is where Mark Fields, president and CEO since 2014, has his office. The main objective of almost everyone who spends any amount of their day up here is to protect his time and attention.

From his penthouse office, Fields looks out and sees the vast expanse of the Ford campus. There's a reason visitors need a car to go to meetings at Ford; it's impossible to cover the campus on foot. Through the windows, the company resembles a little country of engineers making power trains, brakes, and software. To the left is the headquarters of product development; and to the right, the marketing buildings tower over well-kept lawns.

From this singular vantage point, Mark Fields makes decisions that have lasting impact on hundreds of thousands of employees all over the world. But his perspective is fundamentally limited: like most CEOs, he is protected from the world by official and unofficial layers of people. Ford employees will spend months preparing for a one-hour meeting with him, rehearsing over and over again every aspect and responses to every possible question he might have. In ways both direct and indirect, the 199,000 people working for Ford are offering him a highly curated information stream. Some of them are glossing over issues because they don't want to be the bearers of bad news. Others, however, are simply editing out descriptions and details in the name of efficiency. With every single edit in every single conversation, Fields is in danger of losing touch with potent human intelligence that will help him make strategic decisions. And yet, he can't pay attention to everything. Somehow, within these limitations, Fields has to make daily decisions that will determine the future of more than 150 billion dollars in annual revenue.

In the past, he was able to use his intuition to guide him through many of these choices. He has decades of experience in the car industry, including serving as the CEO of Mazda. And, until recently, Ford's model of selling cars—using research and engineering to develop new features to appeal to Ford's mostly American drivers—was a good fit for its buyers. Drivers were eager to pay more money for technologically advanced features, and Ford could use the same marketing that had proved so successful for their very first Model T in 1908: "High Priced Quality in a Low Priced Car." Ford consistently won over drivers with its solid expertise in car engineering—unlike General Motors, Ford has always been a car lover's company. In short, Fields and many of the Ford engineers grew up in the same world as the people buying Ford's cars.

But what happens when people who are living in other worlds start buying Ford's cars? People living in Brazil or China possess strikingly different worldviews, sentiments, and aspirations than do Americans. To these people, Ford's history of solid engineering and middle class values is meaningless. What's more, its specific, high-quality features are often irrelevant or even detriments to the value of the car. Ford had been investing in technologies like Lane Assist—an automated system designed to keep vehicles inside the white lines—but what if their potential drivers live in a Chinese city without clearly demarcated lanes? Ford has explored the idea of driverless cars, but many of their new customers live in places like New Delhi, India, where employing a driver is the norm for car owners and an important way of signifying status.

Faced with a multitude of such problems, the carefully designed spaces and perspectives of an executive like Mark Fields suddenly do not seem so advantageous. He is no longer making decisions based on the knowledge of his own world. He needs to understand the worlds of people in cultures vastly different from his own. What matters to the engineers in Detroit is likely to overlap with what matters to, say, a Texan looking for a truck. But Fields and his engineers at Ford have begun to sense that they don't know enough about what is relevant to a young creative in Shanghai eager to make career and artistic connections, for example, or an entrepreneur in Chennai who is seeking out more space for spiritual reflection in the midst of a grinding work schedule.

When I work with executives like Fields—helping them to discover other cultures and people in emerging markets— they almost always describe their experience in the same way. They can no longer trust their instincts alone as a guiding light for wise decisions. They say, *I've lost my intuition.* And they all want to get it back—quickly. But how?

Gaining the type of understanding that Mark Fields is after— an understanding of other worlds—is only possible with profound insights into culture. And we can't have a meaningful insight into culture if we don't embrace a rigorous and sustained engagement with it. When I use the words "rigorous" and "engagement," I don't mean market research numbers or data analytics. I mean a study of culture that involves the humanities: reading a culture's seminal texts, understanding its languages, getting a firsthand feel for how its people live. Not "76 percent of 21- to 35-year-olds living in urban areas in Brazil buy premium coffee." This kind of data tells us nothing about culture.

Take Starbucks. Yes, the success of the company relies on technology and quantitative analysis: they need the most advanced coffee machines and roasters; they need a streamlined supply chain, well-designed mobile apps, and up-to-date financial technology to drive the company's growth. But the actual heart and soul of the company—its *raison d'être*—is based on a simple but profound cultural insight. Howard Schultz understood how to modify the Southern European coffee culture to the contours of American life. Today all this seems far too obvious, but it was only thirty-five years ago that coffee in North America meant a lukewarm cup of Folgers. Schultz's insight required an understanding of Italian language and culture—he went to Italy and studied the famous Italian coffee bars before taking over at Starbucks—as well as an attunement to an unmet desire in the United States for more shared community spaces.

When we want to understand people—real people in the rich reality of their worlds—we need this type of cultural intelligence. We need to know how their cassoulet smells after an hour in the oven; we need to know that the sand and dirt blowing in their deserts hurts their eyes in the morning; we need to know that their poetry never uses the first-person singular, and that they have always considered their mountains a safe haven when under attack. Investigating a culture in this way—achieving a 360-degree understanding of it—calls on every part of our humanity: we must bring our intellects, our spirits, and all our senses to the task. Most important to remember: if we want to say something meaningful about another culture, we have to let go—just a little bit—of the biases and assumptions that form the scaffolding of our own culture. When we commit to losing a part of ourselves, we gain something profoundly new in exchange. We gain insight. I call the practice of cultivating these types of insights *sensemaking*.

What Is Sensemaking?

Sensemaking is a method of practical wisdom grounded in the humanities. We can think of sensemaking as the exact opposite of algorithmic thinking: it is entirely situated in the concrete, while algorithmic thinking exists in a no-man's-land of information stripped of its specificity. Algorithmic thinking can go wide—processing trillions of terabytes of data per second—but only sensemaking can go deep.

We can trace sensemaking's roots back to Aristotle, the Greek philosopher, who described practical wisdom as *phronesis*. When a highly skilled person exhibits phronesis, it's not just that they possess knowledge of abstract principles and rules. Phronesis is an artful synthesis of both knowledge *and* experience.

In the business world, we see phronesis when skilled traders perform in concert with market conditions and when experienced corporate managers sense subtle changes in organizations involving tens of thousands of people. When a legislative reform is implemented, a politician exhibiting phronesis can envision the chain of events that will play out in every domain of his or her constituency all at once. Many masterful leaders—knowledgeable *and* experienced—describe systems, societies, and organizations as an extension of their body. It is a part of them and they are a part of it.

How do these people achieve such extraordinary results? Though there is no shortcut to this work—no five-step plan, "life hack," or killer PowerPoint to automatically get us there—there are some basic principles that can help all of us stay open to the insights that matter most. These principles are based upon the wealth of theories and methodologies that make up the humanities. I have framed each one of them to sit in direct contradiction to the prevailing assumptions of our algorithmic age.

In the following chapters, I will address each principle in more depth and provide a richer intellectual context for them. We will meet the master practitioners who wrestle with their own interpretations of such a practice based on the following ideas:

The Five Principles of Sensemaking
1. Culture—*not* individuals
2. Thick data—*not* just thin data
3. The savannah—*not* the zoo
4. Creativity—*not* manufacturing
5. The North Star—*not* the GPS

1. Culture—Not *Individuals*

Alice Munro, the Nobel Prize–winning short story writer, once wrote, "It's as if tendencies that seem most deeply rooted in our minds, most private and singular, have come in as spores on the prevailing wind, looking for any likely place to land, any welcome." We like to conceive of ourselves as highly individual, with our own autonomous modes of behaving. Yet, despite the promise of independent thought in modern liberal democracies, our notions of what is appropriate and relevant come to us through social context. As the astute Munro noted, this context determines what shows up as appropriate and relevant—tendencies that travel "like spores."

Why does this matter? If we want to understand the most profound insights of a culture, we must first understand why people in that culture *act* the way they do. That understanding is rarely—if ever—based upon what individual people say or even on what they claim to do. Instead, it is built around an understanding of worlds. Whether we are in the world of hedge fund managers, union employees, artists, mothers, or politicians, we, as humans, are sensitive to how others in our world do things, change things, and think about things.

Philosophy can help us understand this better. Although it is often considered esoteric, philosophy is our greatest intellectual tool for analyzing deeply held cultural assumptions. Martin Heidegger, considered by many to be the greatest philosopher of the twentieth century, overturned all of the presuppositions of Western philosophy when he argued, in 1927, that these unspoken assumptions—the oxygen of our everyday lives—should be called "Being." He defined it as "That on the basis of which beings are understood." This radical new way of conceiving of "us" stood in direct contradiction to the prevailing edicts of rival philospher René Descartes: *I think, therefore I am.* Heidegger's "Being" had nothing to do with an individual thinking, analyzing, or standing at a distance—objectively—from a context.

Heidegger, and the generation of philosophers who followed in his footsteps, argued that there are very few situations—if any—in which the pure, self-contained individual subject has a significant role to play. For this new cadre of philosophers, social context, or "Being," was not just the driver of our everyday behavior; it was the very filter through which reality showed up as intelligible and meaningful. If we were children in the European Middle Ages, for example, our sense of identity and aspiration would necessarily be in relationship to the Church. A young knight in the Middle Ages would experience all phenomena as a reflection of his place next to God. Today, of course, it would never occur to a young man to become a knight—unless as a choice of kitsch or costume. Our reality—everything that we perceive as meaningful—is highly contextual and historical. And most of the time we are incapable of thinking beyond that context. Humans are defined by the society in which they live, Heidegger argued. All of this means that when someone like Mark Fields at Ford wants to understand how to sell cars in places like China, India, and Brazil, he needs a much more nuanced understanding of the social context of these new drivers. And sensemaking is the fastest and most effective means of achieving this type of understanding. To be clear, sensemaking is not a superficial brush-up on the arts—throwing on an album as background music or cruising through a museum exhibit in thirty minutes before going out for a drink. Sensemaking is a demanding form of cultural engagement; its rigor is precisely what makes it so rewarding.

Let me give you a little thought experiment involving two different musicians to illustrate how this works: If you put on jazz great Charlie Parker's Savoy and Dial recordings, you are transported back to Minton's Playhouse club in 1940s Harlem, where the smoke was thick and racial tensions hung heavy in the air. You can hear how his technical proficiency breaks the space-time continuum and, as his playing gets faster and faster, you experience the emergence of an entirely new kind of music called bebop.

If, instead, you put on David Bowie's album *"Heroes"* from 1977 and engage with that one single line "We can be heroes, just for one day," you open yourself up to the desperation of a youth culture infected with cynicism—little in the way of employment or hope for a better future.

Both of these pieces of music offer a direct portal into other worlds. We start to see how reality is structured for a jazz musician in Harlem during World War II and for young people in the post-punk era on the streets of London and New York. Through the nuances of the music, we come to an understanding about the cultural hopes and fears in these specific times and places. We learn what is worth celebrating and what rules—aesthetic, social, or political—need to be broken.

I had a profound experience with this on a recent visit I made to LACMA, the Los Angeles County Museum of Art. I wandered into the room displaying Islamic art from the late Middle Ages and I saw an older man with a worn face sitting on a bench and looking up at a manuscript depicting "The Gathering of Lovers." In the watercolor, brilliantly rendered gold angels surround a figure of Adam, sitting at peace in the center. I stood in the back of the room so as not to disturb the man, but he turned around to speak to me, his face filled with tears. He told me that he was an undocumented worker from Mexico and that he was grieving the death of his mother. He connected with the storytelling in the manuscript painting, he said, because it was clear to him that this artist, working hundreds of years ago in an area of the world utterly foreign to him, had similar wishes for his family. "He wanted them to be in a place of beauty and calm after they died," he told me. And then he thought for a moment before saying, "He must have been just like me."

Great art connects us across the ages. It invites us to empathize with worlds at the very edge of our imaginative horizons. *"...just like me."* At the same time, it can reveal to us the specific assumptions that shape our *own* worlds, our own particular moments in history.

Some cultures prioritize efficiency and order in their meetings, while other cultures use meetings as a way to secure alliances and establish power between players. Lunch is a two-hour feast in some cultures and a ten-minute sandwich in others. Ambition is admired and celebrated in certain circles, and denigrated and mocked in others. These unspoken rules are far away, but so close. They only come to the fore when we keenly observe them or when they break down. It is only when a new hire at work demands an executive title, for example, that company employees become aware of the culture's disdain for hierarchy.

When we practice sensemaking, we stop seeing a room as a space filled with individual items and we start seeing the structures that form a cultural reality. In algorithmic thinking, a bottle of perfume is defined by how many milligrams of liquid exist within it; a pen is a piece of plastic with metal attached to it. In contrast, sensemaking perceives everything in relationship to everything else. The perfume becomes equipment—along with lipstick, high heels, and text messages—in the world of dating. The pen, along with a word processor and paper and books, is part of the world of writing. Pens, perfume, hammers, word processors: everything in our lives has some bearing on everything else. Nothing exists in an individual vacuum.

Philosophers give this concept many names. Pierre Bourdieu would call it "habitus"; Ernesto Laclau and Michel

Foucault referred to it as "the discourse," and still others dubbed it "our conversation" or "the conversation." All of these various thinkers are indebted to Heidegger, who was the first to discover what he called "Being," or background practices.

Although philosophers have been describing this concept for close to a century now, it is too often forgotten or disregarded in our modern world. In realms where quantitative analysis reigns supreme—corporations and financial firms come to mind, as do, increasingly, education and health institutions—these notions of shared worlds and background practices are radical. Just think about the way companies or political campaigns try to understand markets and voters: they ask people what they think. In a focus group or a survey, they take people out of the context of their regular lives and pepper them with questions about discrete ideas, products, or policy ideas. By decontextualizing experiences—pulling worlds apart in an attempt to create an assembly of facts—they miss almost everything that can shed light on human behavior. This is why their conclusions are wrong most of the time.

The concept of "culture—not individuals" serves as an essential corrective to the widely held belief that human behavior is based on individual choices, preferences, and logical structures. We will delve deeper into the structure and importance of shared worlds in Chapter Three.

2. Thick Data—Not Just Thin Data

If sensemaking is interested in cultures, not individuals, it follows, then, that sensemaking data has a completely different texture. A study of French culture, for example, would be dry and technical if it only included data from the Organization for Economic Cooperation and Development (OECD). What about the tactile and visceral pieces of data that communicate so much about French life—a loaf of fresh bread or a glass of Bordeaux? What about reading the poetry of Rimbaud or listening to a song by Serge Gainsbourg? Though these are certainly pursuits that bring us pleasure, they are also pieces of data that are essential to sensemaking.

In 1973, anthropologist Clifford Geertz developed the term *thick description* to characterize his ethnographic field notes. He was interested not just in human behavior but in how that behavior related to the greater cultural context. Geertz spent the lion's share of his academic career writing about the nuances of culturally complex gestures, the *thickness* that adds depth to life. Take the wink as an example: the computer might classify it as a twitch of the eye lasting for a millisecond, but we all know that a wink can mean so much more. This tiny movement has the ability to communicate "I'm not serious," "Let's leave together," "You're an idiot," and so many other, more ineffable messages.

Taking inspiration from Geertz's phrase, I like to call sensemaking data "thick data" because it expresses what is meaningful about a culture. Thick data captures not just facts but the *context* of those facts. Eighty-six percent of households in America drink more than six quarts of milk per week, for example, but *why* do they drink milk? And what is it like? An apple weighing .09 pound and a gram of honey is thin data. A Rosh Hashanah meal with apples dipped in honey, by contrast, is thick data.

Think about it this way: if you are sitting in a chair right now, you know with quite some detail what the sound will be if you push the chair back. What if you drop a piece of paper

from four feet and let it float down until it hits the floor? You
know how it will feel when it leaves your hands; you know that
its fall will be characterized by a gentle wafting back and forth;
you know that it will land silently. Just think for a moment
about all the *stuff you know*. You know when a cup of coffee is
just a touch too cold; you know how it feels outside just before
a thunderstorm; you know something is wrong when you look
in your partner's eyes. Philosophers have called this our famil-
iarity with the world. It is the background upon which we deal
with our lives and go through our days.

This type of knowledge is not a banal fact; it is the very
way we deal with the world. It is how we choose things in the
supermarket, how we cook, read each other, and chop down
a tree. We make sense of the world and get around in it using
this knowledge. It is what AI researchers continually attempt
to copy and inevitably get wrong. This is the knowledge that
makes up thick data.

Because it is not universally applicable like thin data, thick
data is often dismissed as insufficient or lacking rigor. But the
reality is that our lives are dominated by thick data. When we
leave it out of our decisions—or attempt to ignore it—we are
working with a faulty model of humanity. In a business context, this misunderstanding of people can have disastrous consequences. After all, business is almost always about making
bets on human behavior: which product is most likely to sell,
which employee is most likely to succeed, what price is a customer willing to pay. Companies that excel at making these
bets tend to thrive in the marketplace. And the only way to
make these types of killer bets is to understand people better.

Thick data stands in direct contrast with thin data—the

sort of data you get when you look at the traces of our actions and behaviors: we travel this much every day; we search for that on the Internet; we sleep this many hours; we have this many social connections; we listen to this type of music, and so forth. It's the data gathered by the cookies in your browser, the Fitbit on your wrist, or the GPS in your phone. These properties of human behavior are undoubtedly important, but they are not the whole story.

If thin data seeks to understand us based on what we do, thick data seeks to understand us in terms of how we relate to the many different worlds we inhabit. This is precisely why moods are one of our most salient forms of thick data. For example, we can agree, between us, that the mood in the office is dull or the party is just getting started. We can know what it is like to be caught up in the excitement of a sports game or the fervor of a political demonstration. We can all feel the sadness of a cultural moment—"Where were you on 9/11?"—as well as the infectious joy that takes hold when we hear about a courageous act on the news. If our colleague tells us that she feels the organization isn't ready for change right now—*There's too much stress around here*—we nod our heads and agree. When we are attuned to this kind of data, we can sense the subtle but constantly evolving changes of the worlds all around us.

Why is this attunement such an imperative? After all, isn't this what market research and technical reports are for? Despite what people in power *assume*, leaders and key strategic thinkers are almost always surrounded by layers and layers of abstraction. I have watched the faces of many top executives in the corporate world—faces trained to project composure and competence—turn white with shock when confronted with the raw reality of their business, its customers, and the world. Executives who run companies that make shoes often get their own shoes for free—many wouldn't dream of entering a Foot Locker or a DSW. They don't have real data on the reality of going to the shoe store—the problems of price, of presentation, of missing sizes. Many car executives haven't bought their own vehicle since entering the industry. What do they know about the world of their customers? Without this texture of experience, the data shoved before these executives' eyes loses any truth. Context and color are absent; all that remains are abstract representations of the world rather than the world itself.

Simply put, the imaginations and intuitions of top leaders are starving. They have been living on a diet of desiccated facts and figures—thin data stripped of all its organic life. This diet may sustain them through periods of relative stability, but they will likely be headed off course when markets shift. In the midst of changing circumstances, it is vital to reconnect with the emotional—even the visceral—context of humanity. This is where thick data comes in.

3. The Savannah—Not the Zoo

Where do we go to get more thick data? We must start by studying humanity in the full complexity and beauty of the lived world. This is the basis of a philosophical method we will discover called "phenomenology," or the *study of human experiences*. With phenomenology, we are observing human behavior as it exists in social contexts, not in abstract numbers. It's the difference between watching a pack of lions hunt on the actual savannah and seeing them get fed from a bowl in the zoo. The lions are technically eating in both scenarios. Which one do you think holds more truth?

Take the question of love as an example. In 2012, "what is love" was the most searched query on Google. Helen Fisher, a biological anthropologist, offered an answer that received a significant number of hits. Based on fMRI results, Fisher and her colleagues concluded that "romantic love" is not an emotion, but a motivation system—an involuntary chemical reaction. We love because it incentivizes us to engage in relationships with potential mates.

That is what love looks like in the laboratory or the zoo, but Fisher's explanation tells us nothing about how we *experience* love. Historians tell us that romantic love is really only a recent phenomenon. In ancient India, love was seen as dangerously disruptive to social structures, and during the Middle Ages, love was considered akin to insanity. What is love today? Thousands of divorce lawyers would argue against Fischer's explanation of a motivation system. Insights about how love works are only possible by observing what people do and experience in the real world.

The methodology of studying human experience is not interested in what is extraordinary, but what is ordinary and common for all (or most) of us. It isn't about the "r2," or the significant sample size. In fact, a relatively small number of people and their situations will suffice. These experiences should be collected and understood in order to fully see the patterns of behavior we all share. It is a method that brings leadership in actual touch with the people they purport to serve.

Of course, I often hear executives in my world say that they want to help their customers, clients, or employees by finding their "pain points" or "unmet needs." To me, these phrases still communicate an unfortunate distance. They are looking down at people and abstracting their experience from on high. If you want to truly understand the people in your world, you must engage with them at eye level. You must do what they do and see what they see. But even that is not enough. If you really want to understand something about a culture, the trick is to see its ghosts—its artistic heritage, its history, its customs. There is no better training ground for such a perspective than the study of human experience.

4. Creativity—Not Manufacturing

After spending time in the field and engaging with the humanities to better understand the world, how do we achieve actual insights through sensemaking? In which situations is it okay to use a hypothesis and test it out? When is it better not to have any preconceived notions at all? These are different ways of reasoning through a problem: a concern at the center of a centuries-old debate about the scientific method. In the late 1800s, American philosopher and logician Charles Sanders Peirce became famous for defining the three kinds of reasoning we use to solve problems—deduction, induction, and abduction—each one appropriate for different levels of certainty.

Deduction is often called top-down reasoning because it starts with a more general law or theory—a hypothesis—and then attempts to apply it in specific instances. "All women are mortal. Sally is a woman." Therefore we can deduce: "Sally is mortal." Deductive reasoning is useful for constrained problems with set boundaries, but it is unable to incorporate new information.

Inductive reasoning, on the other hand, is the exact opposite of deductive reasoning. It is bottom-up, so it starts with specific observations and then moves up into a theory. "Sally is a doctor." From our observation of Sally, we can then add: "Sally just finished school." And from there, we can infer an explanation or a theory: "Sally graduated from medical school." But when you reason inductively, you have limited yourself to one set of beliefs—all well and good for certain types of problems with set knowns and unknowns—but no longer useful for problems involving culture and behavior. We can observe that Sally is a doctor and then infer that Sally went to medical school, but this framing might not be relevant or meaningful for the problem we are trying to solve. What if we are trying to understand Sally in a completely different cultural context: her world as a mother to small children, or her world as an active member of the local political scene in her town? In these instances, inductive reasoning will shut out possible insights before we even know the context of our investigation.

Peirce contended that only abductive reasoning—or nonlinear problem solving—was capable of generating new ideas. He defined this type of reasoning as a kind of educated guess, appropriate after observing phenomena with no set or logical explanation. Here is a simple example from a series of observations: *A window is broken in the house; the jewelry box is missing; the furniture has been overturned, and there are clothes scattered everywhere.* Through abductive reasoning, we make a *leap* into the most reasonable conclusion: *The house has been robbed.*

For Peirce, abduction was about looking for answers. While the previous few hundred years had been about the development of science and the belief that the industrial age could conquer anything, Peirce, in his *First Rule of Logic* (1899), questioned what we thought we knew. "Do not block the way of inquiry," he said, and he outlined these following four offenses that we commit when we reason:

1. We make an absolute assertion that we're right.
2. We believe something isn't knowable because we don't have the techniques or technologies to figure it out.
3. We insist that some element of science is utterly inexplicable and unknowable.
4. We believe that some law or truth is in its final and perfect state.

Peirce rejected the notion that any theory was "true," while maintaining that it could be "near true." In other words, he believed there was always room for improvement, and endless potential for new truths to emerge.

It's easy to see why scientists would dismiss the idea that you cannot come to the end of something—that facts are not necessarily conclusive. We all want our work to contain some measure of certainty, and living in the constant shadow of doubt is unpleasant. Peirce speaks to this discomfort in his 1877 essay "The Fixation of Belief":

Doubt is an uneasy and dissatisfied state from which we struggle to free ourselves and pass into the state of belief; while the latter is a calm and satisfactory state which we do not wish to avoid, or to change to a belief in anything else.

He ultimately argued that we hold fast to outdated and sometimes downright foolish ideas just to avoid staying in this "uneasy and dissatisfied state." In other words, we often make really poor decisions just because it is so uncomfortable to do the hard work of thinking. And I don't mean thinking in the deductive or inductive sense of the word—reasoning through a problem with a logical and linear set of steps. I mean the type of thinking that leads to all creative insights: filled with twists and turns, dead ends, and unexpected breakthroughs. Abductive reasoning is *messy*. It is extremely difficult for most of us to remain in this state of doubt for an indeterminate amount of time. But doubt is the only state of being that will open us up to new understanding. This is the real story of creativity.

5. The North Star—Not the GPS

We seem to live in an era of unprecedented complexity. Our world tells us that the pace of the seismic change occurring around us has rendered us incapable of seeing the big picture. Whether we are in the TV industry, attempting to navigate the emergence of streaming content providers like Amazon, Hulu, and Netflix, or medical practitioners barraged by an unending stream of often contradictory health studies, it is easy to accept these claims of overwhelming complexity. We want to throw up our hands and turn to the machines all around us: surely big data and algorithmic programming can make some sense of all of this. We, as humans, no longer can.

Allow me to surprise you: I believe that our world is actually no more complex than it has ever been, nor is it more incomprehensible. Yes, we have the Internet and the proliferation of wearable computing, but my grandmother experienced the destruction of two world wars, the discovery of penicillin, and the inventions of mass production, investment banking, and space travel. She lived through the agricultural revolution, witnessing mass starvation followed by a food system that now produces more than enough for everyone (when distributed intelligently). These are only a few of the innovations that utterly transformed her world during her time. Yes, we are living through change. Is it seismic? My grandmother would say, "Not really."

Today's world feels overwhelmingly complex because we are obsessed with organizing it as an assembly of facts. Big data makes us feel as though we can and should know everything there is to know on earth. But this is a fool's quest, and it leaves everyone involved feeling depleted and lost. We are so fixated on staring at the oracle of the GPS that we have lost all sensitivity to the stars shining right above our heads. The tools of navigation have always been available to all of us. But we must take responsibility for *interpreting* them. This means executives need to be prepared to understand new and unfamiliar contexts—political, technological, cultural—and to interpret their place in our increasingly interdependent world.

Therein lies sensemaking's greatest offering: it teaches us two essential things about leadership in an era of big data. To begin with, sensemaking can guide us in selecting an appropriate context for data collection. After all, the mere task of collecting data is meaningless in the abstract. What data do we collect? What for? How? It is impossible to study the world without some sort of paradigm for thinking about what you want to study.

Secondly, sensemaking shows us how to cultivate a perspective on how data fits together as an expressive portrait. Leaders must find a team who can use data to piece together a richly textured view of the world, in which resulting interpretations can add up to something greater than the data collected.

In this way, sensemaking teaches us where to put our attention. We don't try to know everything; we work to make sense of something. In the midst of complexity, a sensemaking practice allows us to determine what actually matters.

The business of food products, for example, is not just about market entry plans, capital investment, and product positioning. It is about understanding how we, as a culture, sit in relationship to food. How we consume it; how we share it; what it means to us. Strategy is about finance but also about culture, people, emotions, behavior, and needs.

Instead of attempting to reduce the complexity of all of these layers of humanity—like a journey determined by the reductions of a GPS—the sensemaking practice follows the North Star. We learn to navigate through the rich reality of our world, developing a finely honed perspective on where we are and where we are headed. If algorithmic thinking offers us the illusion of objectivity—or a view from nowhere—then sensemaking allows us determine where we are. And, most important, sensemaking puts us in touch with where we are headed.

Before we can begin the journey, however, it is important to situate ourselves more specifically in the culture that vehemently advances the tenets of an algorithmic understanding of the world. Nowhere is this belief more widely held than in

"Silicon Valley." I write the name in quotes because I am not just referring to the strip of land in the southern San Francisco Bay Area. Silicon Valley is now an ideology, a mindset that values knowledge from the hard sciences above all other forms of knowing. Its cultural prerogatives have now seeped into every aspect of our modern life, including business, education, health care, media, and government. We cannot talk about the urgency of sensemaking without first making a stop to more fully dismantle the assumptions upheld in a Silicon Valley state of mind.

Chapter Two

Silicon Valley Is a State of Mind

"Data! Data! Data!" he cried impatiently. "I can't make bricks without clay!"

—*Arthur Conan Doyle,* The Adventure of the Copper Beaches

The library will endure; it is the universe. As for us, everything has not been written; we are not turning into phantoms. We walk the corridors, searching the shelves and rearranging them, looking for lines of meaning amid leagues of cacophony and incoherence, reading the history of the past and our future, collecting our thoughts and collecting the thoughts of others, and every so often glimpsing mirrors, in which we may recognize creatures of the information.

—*Jorge Luis Borges, "The Library of Babel"*

In a 2013 conference call with Wall Street analysts, Mark Zuckerberg told investors that, along with prioritizing increased connectivity across the globe and emphasizing a knowledge economy, Facebook was committed to a new vision called "understanding the world." He described what this "understanding" would soon look like: "Every day, people post billions of pieces of content and connections into the graph [Facebook's algorithmic search mechanism], and in doing this, they're helping to build the clearest model of everything there is to know in the world."

This is only one of many grandiose claims coming out of Silicon Valley right now. Google's mission statement is famously to "organize the world's information and make it universally accessible and useful." In a 2013 interview in *Fortune*, Jeremiah Robison, the vice president of software at Jawbone, explained that the goal with their fitness tracking device Jawbone UP was "to understand the science of behavior change." Jack Dorsey, of Twitter and Square Inc. fame, told a room full of entrepreneurs that start-ups are following in the footsteps of Gandhi and the Founding Fathers. In a 2014 press release, Uber's CEO and cofounder Travis Kalanick announced that with Uber's "growth and expansion, the company has evolved from being a scrappy Silicon Valley tech start-up to being a way of life for millions of people in cities around the world." With this work, "we fight the good fight."

In contrast to the persistent narrative of American economic malaise and political gridlock, the Silicon Valley vision provides an infusion of hope and optimism. As a result, the reigning ethos of Silicon Valley has grown popular in American cultural life, assuming a greater role as our attachment to our technological devices has grown, and more and more of our daily life happens on the Internet. Like any community, Silicon Valley has a strong shared culture and outlook, one that it credits for its success. Its well-worn mantras have now seeped into mainstream discourse: everything from the "sharing economy" to "leapfrogging" to "fail forward" to the "lean start-up." Despite the different phrases, the ideology remains the same. The promise is that technology will solve it—whatever *it* is. And the solution is sure to be revolutionary. No one in Silicon Valley ever launches a start-up by saying, "We will make small, incremental changes in the field of X based on all of the small, incremental changes that have been made over the last five decades." Everything is a disruption: a clean break from the past leaning far forward into the future.

The culture has upended the way we educate our children, the way we do our business, and the way we conceive of ourselves as citizens. In the process, Silicon Valley either belittles humanities-based education or renders it irrelevant to the work of the twenty-first century. Influential venture capitalist Marc Andreessen reflects this way of thinking when he argued in his 2014 blog post "Culture Clash" that the liberal arts are behind the cultural curve. "For people who aren't deep into math and science and technology," he wrote, "it is going to get far harder to understand the world going forward." PayPal founder and investor Peter Thiel went so far as to establish the Thiel Fellowship, which pays young entrepreneurs to forgo university studies so that they might fast-track their start-up projects.

So what *is* valued in this state of mind? Let's critique some of the main assumptions at play in this ideology so we can better understand the way it is changing our notions of an intellectual life. In a "Silicon Valley" state of mind, sensemaking has never been more lacking or more urgently needed.

Assumptions behind Disruptive Innovation

There is a lot of talk about "disruption" in Silicon Valley. Successful entrepreneurs upend traditional ways of doing things; they "disrupt" a market, rather than simply selling a product. When we unpack the assumption implicit in this "disruption," we gain a keen insight into the way that Silicon Valley thinks about innovation and progress. Disrupting an industry, in Silicon Valley parlance, suggests a clean break between "before" and "after." This reflects scientific thinking, wherein a hypothesis is presented and it is regarded as operational and "true" until it is shown to be false, or is superseded. As long as that hypothesis holds up to scrutiny, it takes precedence over all previous work. This, of course, is temporary; a new hypothesis will eventually take its place. It's a discipline that's always moving forward.

This way of thinking stands in sharp contrast to the intellectual tradition of the humanities, which does not suggest clean breaks in knowledge, and does not regard past experience as outmoded or outdated. Instead, it focuses on the ways in which dominant powers and attitudes shape contemporary culture, and the possibility of recovery of knowledge and understanding that have been obscured (either intentionally or not) by the passage of time or the distance of space. As T. S. Eliot wrote in his 1940 poem "East Coker": "There is only the fight to recover what has been lost / And found and lost again and again."

But Silicon Valley culture feels that the humanities have little relevance to professional life. To disrupt is to reject what has come before. Silicon Valley wants a radical break with accumulated knowledge. Because this "disruption" reflects a widely held belief that innovation requires a fearless willingness to change and a break with the past, is it almost exclusively associated with youth. Silicon Valley celebrates inexperience because it makes it easier to take risks. Mark Zuckerberg summed up a popular attitude when he told attendees at a Stanford event in 2007 that "young people are just smarter." Echoing this idea, venture capitalist Vinod Khosla told the audience at a 2011 tech event in Bangalore that "people over forty-five basically die in terms of new ideas." In this environment, rejection of traditional intellectual life is de rigueur. An unnamed analyst told *New Yorker* journalist George Packer, "If you're an engineer in Silicon Valley, you have no incentive to read *The Economist*."

One way this attitude manifests itself is in an obsession with quantification, which for the youth of Silicon Valley is a stand-in for the knowledge of wisdom and experience. Quantification takes many forms, among them the "quantified self" movement, where adherents use devices to track and quantify aspects of their behavior. It also reflects a broad trend in American society toward quantification: in health care in education, in government, in our personal lives. This is now familiar to us through the term *big data*.

Assumptions behind Big Data

Big data concerns itself with correlation, not causation. It can establish a statistically significant relationship, but it cannot explain *why* it is so. And with increasingly large data sets, there is an increased risk of misleading statistically significant correlations—it can appear that there are many needles in a very large haystack. Big data offers information without explanations for it. As economist and journalist Tim Hartford put it in a 2014 article for the *Financial Times,* "Big data does not solve the problem that has obsessed statisticians and scientists for centuries: the problem of insight, of inferring what is going on, and figuring out how we might intervene to change a system for the better."

What happens when big data is used instead of traditional research methods, rather than alongside them? The case of Google Flu Trends provides us with a salient example. In 2008, researchers at Google wanted to explore the idea of using search terms to predict widespread outbreaks of illness. By isolating flu-related queries on Google and tracking them, the researchers postulated that they could predict an outbreak of the flu sooner than the data from the Centers for Disease Control and Prevention. Using a technique they dubbed "nowcasting," the researchers put their theory into action and published the results in *Nature.* By all accounts, it seemed like a grand success. The Google queries were predicting flu outbreaks two weeks sooner than data coming from the CDC.

And then Google Flu Trends started to fail. It missed the entire H1N1 pandemic in 2009 and wildly overestimated flu outbreaks in the 2012–13 season. In a two-year period ending in 2013, scientists estimated that Google Flu Trends predictions were high in 100 out of 108 weeks. What went wrong? Among other problems, Google's algorithm was vulnerable to any queries that were related to flu *season* but not related to actual flu outbreaks. Therefore, searches like "high school basketball" and "chicken soup" ticked off a flu warning—correlation by pure chance with no real causal relationship to a case of the flu. This is because big data doesn't care about explaining *why.* Instead, it reflects an empiricist's mindset. Big data wants to remove human bias from the equation, embracing deductive thinking and jettisoning inductive modes of inquiry. With enough data, the numbers speak for themselves and you don't need theory. But, as we discovered in the case of Google Flu Trends, deeper analysis is required for correlations to have implications, and to establish causality. Big data cannot simply shake off its reliance on traditional research methods; its meaning still comes out of its interpretation. Try as Silicon Valley might, big data will never be neutral.

Despite examples like Google Flu Trends that expose the limitations of big data, Silicon Valley's data evangelists continue to proselytize. They base their arguments on a now-legendary 2008 *Wired* magazine article entitled "The End of Theory" by Chris Anderson. According to the article's argument, the way we explained systems in the past—through models and hypotheses—is becoming an increasingly irrelevant, crude approximation to the truth. In 2008, the Internet, smartphones, and CRM software were already delivering a superabundance of data. "The numbers speak for themselves," Anderson wrote as he quoted business leaders like Peter Norvig, director of research at Google. "All models are wrong, and increasingly you can succeed without them." Ultimately, Anderson took Norvig's ideas and went to town with them:

This is a world where massive amounts of data and applied mathematics replace every other tool that might be brought to bear. Out with every theory of human behavior, from linguistics to sociology. Forget taxonomy, ontology, and psychology. Who knows why people do what they do? The point is they do it, and we can track and measure it with unprecedented fidelity. With enough data, the numbers speak for themselves.

These companies have embraced a teleology of data, where more data will yield progressively more: better results for consumers, a more accurate understanding of consumers' needs and wants, and better outcomes for society at large. But is bigger really better?

Understanding the world with a sample size in the millions is a radical departure from other types of inquiry. Big data may tell us something about people, but it can tell us precious little about individual persons. How much truth about a situation can Silicon Valley tell us, for example, if it doesn't acknowledge that human behavior is always embedded in a context?

Nineteenth-century pragmatist William James critiqued this naïve approach to data when he responded to the reductionists of his era. In his 1890 book, *The Principles of Psychology*, James wrote: "No one ever had a simple sensation by itself. Consciousness...is of a teeming multiplicity of objects and relations." A white swan seems red in a red light; to understand the color of swans, we also have to understand the properties of light. Facts, in other words, always live in a context, and hacking them into discrete data points renders them meaningless and incomplete.

Assumptions behind Frictionless Technology

One popular concept in Silicon Valley is "frictionless" technology. It's the standard for innovation in the Valley. Technology can be deemed frictionless when it operates smoothly and intuitively, without requiring any human input in the form of thoughts or emotions. In these instances, technology becomes a seamless part of real life. But what do these sorts of technologies mean for human thought and effort? Should we all take for granted the role of technology in our lives, or are there times and situations where we want a more thoughtful engagement with the technology we use? As Silicon Valley's way of thinking about frictionless technology grows popular, it will shape the kind of innovation that people think is exciting, and the work that merits funding and study, narrowing—rather than expanding—our sense of possibility.

In a 2010 interview in the *Wall Street Journal,* Google's then-CEO Eric Schmidt argued, "Most people don't want Google to answer their questions . . . they want Google to tell them what they should be doing next." This reflects a subtle shift in the culture of the Internet, and in Western culture and public life more broadly, that should raise red flags. When we search on Google or post on Facebook, the ever-changing algorithms that underpin these platforms shape the information we get about our friends, about what's going on in the world, about our health and well-being. In ways that people overlook, Silicon Valley shapes the information we get access to, all in the name of tailoring it more effectively to our needs and preferences.

One oft-made point is that this personalization leads to polarization. By feeding people content that reflects their views and shielding them from people they may disagree with, filtering mechanisms make the public sphere less and less dynamic. Internet activist Eli Pariser dubbed this the "filter bubble."

The dangers of "frictionless technology" lie not in what it can or cannot do for us, but in how it shapes our thinking. Why seek out new information, why learn something different, or push the boundaries of debate or previously accepted ideas, when data can serve up exactly what reflects already-established outlooks and preferences? This is what journalists, commentators, and political analysts have dubbed the "post-truth era." In a Silicon Valley state of mind, we care less about actively seeking out the truth than we do about engaging in discourse and experiences that make us feel affirmed and acknowledged.

It goes without saying that there are tremendous benefits to all of the innovations happening in both the real Silicon Valley and in its culture at large. No one is arguing for completely doing away with all of the cutting-edge technology or the spirit of entrepreneurship that makes this culture such a prominent player in our global economy. The critique here is of Silicon Valley's quiet, creeping costs on our intellectual life. The humanities, or our tradition of describing the rich reality of our world—its history, politics, philosophy, and art—are being denigrated by every assumption at play in Silicon Valley.

When we believe that technology will save us, that we have nothing to learn from the past or that numbers can speak for themselves, we are falling prey to dangerous siren songs. We are seeking out silver bullet answers instead of engaging in the hard work of piecing together the truth.

Sensemaking is a corrective to all of these misguided assumptions of Silicon Valley. Even with the magnificent computational power now at our disposal, there is no alternative to sitting with problems, stewing in them, and struggling through them with the help of careful, patient human observation. In the chapters to follow, I will reveal the road map for how to do just that.

Chapter Three

Culture—Not Individuals

Society is something that precedes the individual. Anyone who either cannot lead the common life or is so self-sufficient as not to need to, and therefore does not partake of society, is either a beast or a god.

—*Aristotle*, Politics

After examining the assumptions of the ideology so prevalent in Silicon Valley, one would think that companies and organizations in today's world would feel a relative sense of confidence about making big bets on human behavior. With massive data sets now available through machine learning and a potential model of "everything there is to know in the world" in the making, what more is there left to ponder? Human behavior: it's in the bag.

The reality, of course, is that businesses and organizations are often in a fog about how to move forward through moments of great change. Leadership has lost the ability to imagine and intuit how the world—and their own business or institution—might be evolving.

Through my consulting work with my company, ReD Associates, I spend much of my time in the belly of these types of organizations—some of the most troubled companies on the planet. When I say "troubled," I don't mean that these companies are necessarily losing market share or that they are struggling in the midst of internal power dynamics—although both of these things are often true. What I mean by "troubled" is that the entire culture inside the organization is seized by a mood of directionless panic. The Germans have a word that perfectly describes this mood: *Scheue*. It refers to the moment a horse is stung by a wasp. *Scheue* succinctly captures the atmosphere of flailing attempts at action amid an indecipherable deluge of data points.

Of course, major corporations are not the only cultures that experience *Scheue*. Think about our own responses as individuals to a crisis like climate change. We are filled with anxiety about it, but we often have no idea how to move forward in any meaningful, strategic way. Some of us muck about in the science, trying to piece together a plan of effective action, while most of us simply walk around paralyzed, stricken late at night with a growing sense of fear and dread.

Sensemaking offers us a path forward through this type of fear and dread. The analytical tools I bring to the table are culled from an engagement with disciplines like philosophy, anthropology, literature, history, and the arts. And the very first place I start when I take on a new corporate client is always with an understanding of the world.

When I say "the world," I mean the world of the customers and the competitors, of course. But first, and much more fundamentally, I mean an understanding of the world of the company itself. How is reality constructed inside any one company or another? What assumptions are widely held? Why do people do things? Does the world reward those who challenge orthodoxy? Is it a world where people are curious about the products they sell? How do their work streams flow from one department to another? All of these questions—and so many more—make up the world of the company.

If you are an accountant, or a brand manager, or a corporate lawyer, chances are you walk through the doors of your company's headquarters and things appear relatively orderly. They seem to make sense. But if you are interested in worlds—an analysis culled from the humanities—it is often absurd what is happening in the middle of such cultures. I routinely see companies investing money in things for no other reason than that they have always invested money in such things; they also routinely cut things that are vital to the heart and the soul of the entire company. These types of decisions are made because the numbers add up—streamlining is deemed necessary or they are benchmarking their goals against competitors—but the decisions make no sense to anyone observing the *reality* of the company's world. In fact, such decisions—in the midst of a highly uncertain climate—can be detrimental enough to completely undermine a company's future.

This is an important distinction: the difference between a holistic understanding of a world versus a more atomized understanding of rows of numbers in a spreadsheet. The humanities put us in touch with this more holistic perspective. What is it *like* to work in this company? Or to use its products? Philosophy, again, can guide us in our understanding of how these different realities are constructed. As we discussed earlier in

Chapter One, this distinction points to a philosophical debate that has been going on for two thousand years. What does it mean to be human: what does it mean to be *us*? If, for example, you are a philosopher following in the tradition of Descartes— "I think, therefore I am"—you assume that reality is constructed through a rational and analytical thought process. We are human because we *think*. In other words, humanity is at its best when it is approaching the world from an abstract and theoretical perspective.

But more recently, over the last century, philosophers in continental Europe have broken away from this analytical understanding of our realities. The different thinkers who make up the phenomenological tradition were more interested in a contextual understanding of humanity. We are human because of the way we exist within different social contexts. This philosophy argued that it was our ability to understand and care about our shared worlds that actually makes us human, rather than the ability to sit, like Descartes, and "think about" life as though seeing it through a window.

In a sensemaking process, we are not trying to find out what people "think" about things. Opinions and perceptions are largely irrelevant. Instead, our grounding in the humanities allows us to go deeper. We are interested in uncovering the structures that govern different realities. Heidegger, at the forefront of this phenomenological tradition, argued for a view of experience—not to mention people—as inextricable worlds, in which we cannot separate mind from body, person from environment. The phenomenologists did not aim to dismantle the scientific method as a tool for understanding physics or science—rather, they claimed that these methods simply weren't sufficient for making sense of people.

Heidegger argued that the main topic we should all study is "that on the basis of which beings are understood." What is holding the world together? What are the assumptions underlying what people are doing?

Why does this distinction between Cartesian and phenomenological philosophy matter? After all, we are not academics in a philosophy department. What difference does it make to all of us in our daily lives? Many of you probably already agree—yes, we exist within a social context; so what? I am here to tell you that this distinction—our erroneous understanding of humanity—has wide-ranging implications for all aspects of our lives. When we get our understanding of humanity wrong, we get everything wrong. When I walk into a corporation in the midst of a crisis, all sorts of different people will tell me all sorts of different things about what they *think*. Then they hand me memos and other paper containing even more of their thinking. And then these are followed by reams of quantitative data about what their customers and their competitors think—often arriving in gigabytes. This is a vast quantity of data on "thinking"—analysis culled from a Cartesian understanding of humanity—but it is essentially meaningless without studying the *world*. What underlies everything? What holds it all together? Based on what are these people doing and saying these things? Only when we engage in an investigation of these questions can we find a way forward that makes sense.

This is precisely what the Ford Motor Company discovered when they took an immersive dive into the world of their drivers.

The Smell of Lincoln

In one of Ford's many dozen buildings on their corporate campus, there is an innocuous corridor ending in a flight of stairs down to the basement level. Once downstairs, however, a veritable car graveyard is revealed. This cavernous space—resembling a boiler room—is where the Ford engineers dismantle their competitors' cars. Shells of former cars are lined up while their ripped-out components sit in piles nearby. Tires and alloy wheels that have been crash-tested and burnt up are strewn across the floor, and barrels with labels like "oily rags" and "used auto parts" line the walls.

Amid the dusty floors, neon lights, and growling noises, there is a hulking steel door. And from behind that door, a beautiful, warm white light floods out into the car graveyard. In this pristine white room tucked into the basement, Ford has created a choreographed storyboarding experience that explores the "Future of Lincoln," their luxury car brand, in the year 2030. The signature smell of Lincoln—the citrusy scent in all Lincoln dealerships—wafts out from behind the doors into the engineering bowels of the entire company. This is the smell of luxury, and Ford wants more of it.

Unless you live in Detroit, you could be forgiven for assuming the Lincoln luxury brand disappeared years ago. It's not a name that comes up often in car talk these days. In 2015, Lincoln actually had its strongest sales earnings in more than six years—they reported 101,000 vehicles sold—but Lincoln is still trailing far behind Cadillac, its arch nemesis in Detroit. German rivals like BMW, Mercedes, and Audi are so far ahead in sales, they barely even bother to bring up Lincoln in their competitive market analysis.

How far the brand has fallen from its early days in the middle of the twentieth century. It all started when Edsel Ford, the chief of the Ford Motor Company, toured Europe in 1938. He returned to Detroit with a vision for a car that was "strictly continental." Famed car designer E. T. "Bob" Gregorie was up to the task, and by the 1940s the new Continentals were rolling off the assembly lines and into the driveways of America's most famous jet-setters. For the next two decades, everyone from Elvis Presley to Elizabeth Taylor to Frank Sinatra owned a Lincoln. But it was 1961 when the Lincoln Continental came into its own. The new model was the culmination of designer Elwood Engel's legendary career, leaving an indelible mark on the American psyche when JFK was shot in his black Lincoln on a tour through Dallas.

By the 1970s and '80s, however, Ford lost its feel for the luxury car market. Their sleek designs gave way to kitsch, often with standard Ford engineering—not luxury—underneath. Lincoln continued to lose ground to the U.S. market newcomers like Mercedes and BMW, as well as to their original hometown rival Cadillac. By the '90s, they were even losing customers to other Ford products. The Ford Fusion and a reimagined Taurus—now offering a wide variety of luxury features—both started to encroach on Lincoln's vastly diminished share of the luxury market.

Today, the once-storied brand holds just 5.5 percent of the luxury car market, and the average age of its customer base is 65. Lincoln has become a liability; executives within in the company even considered killing it off entirely. How could they begin to make the brand relevant again?

———— ⌇ ————

To fully answer that question, we must first go back to the most fundamental principle of sensemaking: an understanding of worlds. Taking our cue from Heidegger, we start by exploring "that on the basis of which beings are understood." This is an examination of the world of luxury cars and their drivers, but also of the culture of Ford itself. How does the Ford culture conceive of the driving experience? And how is that different from the reality of the world of its customers?

To begin with, Ford is a company with a long history of engineering excellence. They have always taken tremendous pride in making great cars and exceeding drivers' expectations. They want people to love their cars and they work hard to deliver on that promise to their customers. But the way they work—*that on the basis of which*—is driven by engineering and technological innovations. It has everything to do with the world of car engineers and not much to do with the world of their drivers. Henry Ford famously said, "If I had asked people what they wanted, they would have said faster horses." This statement articulates the assumption at the heart of the Ford culture: technological features and options make driving meaningful. The result of this assumption—the "basis on which"—meant that different engineers working within Ford would improve upon their specific component—the navigation system, say—based largely on their own white, male, middle-class Michigan view of what drivers want from a navigation system. Throughout the process, all of these individual car engineering components would come together into the vehicle. Meanwhile, the Ford engineers would work to make it all seem cohesive and appealing.

Of course, like any other major global corporation, Ford had a surfeit of research on Lincoln's market share and its current and intended consumer base. If they had any hope of reviving Lincoln and making it a relevant luxury brand, they needed to reach a particular class of consumers: younger, better educated, more globally minded and creative than the existing consumer group of Lincoln drivers. Unlike the emerging middle-class drivers of twenty or thirty years ago in places like China and India, these young drivers are securely in the upper middle class. They were raised in material comfort, so they are circumspect about flashy conspicuous consumption. For them, the word *luxury* means something completely different. Ford's understanding of where the majority of luxury car buyers will be in thirty years relies on their strategic grasp of what that "something different" amounts to.

The company's research accurately captured the thin data of this demographic—what they "thought" about—as well as many useful statistics about their bodies behind the wheel, such as their weight and ergonomics. But Ford had limited understanding of the *world* of these consumers: the way they constructed their reality. Sensemaking provided the missing connective tissue.

We partnered with Ford to conduct a large-scale ethnographic research project to explore the driving experience for this particular group. This started by studying the group in cities in the United States and China. Though the research was clear that the future of the luxury car market was also moving to India and Russia, leadership at Ford initially resisted the idea of conducting research there. This is a testament to the conflicting priorities that exist inside every large corporation. Including these emerging markets made sense for the long-term strategic goals—in thirty years, every luxury carmaker will want a stronghold in India—but the short-term pressures of time and resources still made it a challenging proposition.

When all of the pieces of the study were in place, our researchers set out to study sixty subjects in cities in the United States, China, India, and Russia. Once there, they created "vehicle ecologies" to describe the complex network of social structures that existed around each and every driver. They spent time with wives, husbands, sisters, brothers, neighbors, and friends. Over the course of half a year, they created a rich web of understanding around each one of the sixty subjects. After researchers had tracked and coded all of the information contained in their field notes, photographs, interviews, journal entries, and other forms of qualitative data gathering, one pattern became strikingly clear: the future of the car had very little to do with the actual experience of driving. The researchers noted that 95 percent of the time, cars were not being used—either sitting in the garage or on the street. And most of the remaining 5 percent of *actual* driving time was spent in the tedium of traffic. Ironically, Ford's engineering focus on driving left a lot of consumers dissatisfied because driving was such a small part of their car experience. The drivers Ford intends to woo are basically in permanent gridlock.

If their relationship to the car is no longer just about the driving and luxury is not a brand or flashy gold plates on a bumper, what creates meaning inside the vehicle? What do they seek out from their experience inside—as well as outside—the car? Sensemaking's ability to reveal the structure of their worlds provided the essential understanding into what this new kind of "car experience" might look like.

One 37-year-old participant from Moscow described the freedom of feeling carefree on his solo car trips. He created a ritual of blasting Russian hip-hop and jamming with his hands on the dashboard—things he wouldn't dream of doing anywhere else but in the context of the car. His story—and others like it—revealed that luxury is an experience of self-expression in a completely private space. A 38-year-old woman in Bombay told researchers how much she cherished time in the car with her closest friends and family. "When we go to Goa," she said, "we really enjoy driving when it is dark. Just sitting in the glowing light together is so nice. It is a pleasure." Her observations and experiences paralleled others in the study. Her vision articulated the luxury of experiencing bonding, hospitality, and meaningful connections in a beautifully designed space. For other members of the group, such as a 31-year-old diamond jeweler from Mumbai, luxury is a mobile office suite that allows ambitious business owners to dote on clients coming in from out of town. "Making the client experience seamless helps my business to flourish," he told the researchers.

All total, sensemaking revealed a handful of specific experiences that these consumers are seeking out: everything from more stylish opportunities for bonding to spaces for private expression to contexts for a more intense focus and productivity. This detailed understanding of different worlds gave Lincoln a new set of high-level objectives, delivering something holistic to the driver that had nothing to do with the grain of the leather or the optics on the headlights. Ford realized that luxury *experiences* needed to drive the design and engineering process: a total transformation in how a company like Ford conceives of the car.

Once Ford started to focus on these experiences, there was no way to consider any of the devices in the car in isolation. Objects—be they a window button, a steering wheel, or an anti-lock braking system—function within relational worlds, what we might call "chains of meaning." We can even extend this idea further by saying that all tools, all pieces of equipment—the stuff that surrounds us—are a system for our "in order to's." A hammer is only a hammer when it is used in order to a build a house in order to create a shelter in order to have a home in order to feel secure. I drink Coke in order to stay awake in order to be productive in order to be successful in order to provide for my loved ones.

Consider an example from a Chinese man who participated in the study: his family had an espresso-style coffee machine. That would not be remarkable in Italy or in the United States, but in China, with such a long and rich tea culture, coffee drinkers are less common. This family would go on adventures to places like Sumatra to seek out rare coffee beans and bring them home to share. This type of quest was the organizing principle for their time together. In "chains of meaning," they sought out rare coffee beans *in order to* feel like open-minded and curious people *in order to* feel like the best versions of themselves *in order to* feel fully alive.

To truly understand Ford's radical reimagining of the luxury car design process, it is helpful to examine what other luxury vehicles are currently promising their drivers. In a Mercedes or Audi, for example, the entire design language of the car—the muscular rear hips that resemble a cat about to pounce and the prominent front dashboard—tell an adrenaline-infused story of a driver zooming forward like a jet pilot. These are the general assumptions of the luxury car market: drivers want speed and thrill.

Like Ford, these carmakers are also struggling to translate the fantasy of the open road into the reality of a future with a driverless car. The response from most of Ford's competitors is to offer up a vision of productivity inside the car. If luxury car owners are not actually driving, then they must be working. The renderings of these luxury vehicles often show three or four people sitting in swiveling white car seats with generic buttons and screens surrounding them—labels like "social media" and "Bluetooth" are prominently displayed. This vision of "work" feels comical precisely because it is so generic and devoid of context. They are attempting to transplant domains wholesale from other worlds—taking the world of the office, for example—and plop them into the car.

In Volvo's cars, the promise of driverless technology is even more vague. Their renderings always show people staring straight ahead at the dashboard. They no longer need to drive, but Volvo has no compelling vision for what that freedom might offer. Their prototypical passengers seem to be in the midst of an existential crisis, paralyzed by the prospect of their new freedom in the car.

Whereas other luxury car brands were telling the story of an aggressive experience on the exterior—racing down the freeway at 150 miles per hour desperately trying to control an overpowered vehicle—with an abstract conceit about "work" on the inside, Ford is prioritizing an understanding of real people and their experiences of being in and using a vehicle. From there, innovation and engineering follow.

Of course, it is impossible to speak about this kind of sensemaking without also acknowledging the role of leadership in major strategy shifts. Sensemaking revealed that if Ford wanted to revamp Lincoln, they needed to completely reorganize their entire corporate structure. This would mean rerouting the path of a company that is the size of a small country, an organization with thousands of employees and a rich history embedded in American culture for more than a century. Such a moment calls for inspired and courageous leadership, and Mark Fields was up to the task. In the midst of the Lincoln story, Fields was already exploring how best to bring Ford into a future of driverless cars. He could sense that the existing industrial structure focused around features was no longer relevant. By letting technology and engineering lead the innovation, the entire company was becoming out of touch with its actual consumers.

In tandem with other strategic shifts occurring in Ford, Fields used the sensemaking insights to drive the reorganization of jobs and processes across the entire company. Employees no longer think of themselves as "working on technology." Instead, their work is focused on "how technology serves people and their experiences." And the American consumer—along with the culture of Detroit—has ceased to be the sole perspective. Fields is using sensemaking insights culled from a variety of studies to globalize the outlook of the entire company, doing away with abstract units like "customers" and "users" and shifting into conversations around dealers, drivers, and passengers.

In the coming years, Fields is rallying around one strategic goal: The Ford Motor Company will innovate entirely around the experiences of actual people and their worlds. As a result of this, "the car"—once the company's raison d'être—is becoming just one object in entire series of relational worlds. Ford is shifting from being an automaker into a hybrid technology and transportation services company. And Mark Fields is at the helm to keep the company cohesive while they navigate away from Detroit into this brave new world.

Despite what we may think, we are not individuals; what we say often has very little bearing on our actual behavior. We are, all of us, situated in a context. If we are to understand human behavior, then we must understand context, an argument for the holistic versus the atomized. A car is just an object; we cannot interpret anything about its driver until we have access to the chains of meaning that connect the driver to a social world.

The more we understand about worlds—and the ways in which social contexts pull our actions out of us—the more we can appreciate what it means to develop interpretive skills. Later in this chapter, I will discuss how we move from proficiency to mastery in this skill building.

First, however, I want to tell you a brief story about a woman I met named Nicole Pollentier. I share her story with you because it perfectly illustrates how we acquire skills and meaning in our lives through our shared contexts. I liken it to an emotional proof of the existence of worlds, a bulwark against mainstream culture's increasing attempts to atomize, quantify, and reduce the depth of our knowledge. Ironically enough, though this story offers a testament to the power of the humanities, its subject matter comes to us straight from the annals of brain science.

How to Make Tamales

It was the winter of 2012 and Nicole Pollentier was taking a trip to Target. For most of the shoppers around her, it couldn't have been a more mundane experience. This particular Target in Pittsburgh had the same cherry-red bull's eye, the same big-bin shopping carts. For Pollentier, however, the simple errand was a momentous event. Only two months before, she had suffered a traumatic brain injury after falling down a flight of cement stairs. The outing to Target was her first attempt to navigate the world outside of her apartment and her doctors' offices since her accident on November 4, 2011.

Subdural hemorrhage; subarachnoid hemorrhage; skull fractures; temporal bone and basilar skull fractures. These phrases formed the new language Pollentier used to describe her current condition to her neurologists as well as to herself. Her working memory, or the holding and processing of new or already stored information, was particularly impaired. "Your working memory is like a waiting room," Pollentier told me. "Everything comes in here and the brain determines what is important and what is not important, making decisions instantaneously about what should be discarded. If something is deemed important, the brain then decides if it's important in five minutes or in five years."

Up until her brain injury, Pollentier was an accomplished poet, so this "waiting room"—her working memory—was essential to her work. "Even as a kid," she told me, "I could feel when my brain was remembering things for poetry later on. I would see things as all aglow and when they entered my little waiting room, there was a 'ding ding ding.' They were stored in the poetry-making section. That always felt very different than the 'remember car registration' section."

But Pollentier's brain damage made it next to impossible for her to engage in poetry making. The injury was so severe, in fact, that she found it difficult to complete even the most routine of errands—Target, for example. "I walked in that store and I just started to cry. The sensory overload: it was so confusing. Like when kids get really excited but the excitement turns into tears and exhaustion all of a sudden. All I could do was stand in the aisle and cry."

Pollentier returned to her apartment and, for several months, she left only to see doctors—neurologists, neuro-psychiatrists, and other brain specialists. Not only was she incapable of writing poetry, she couldn't even remember some of her favorite poetry and song lyrics. "I would remember one phrase from lyrics and then everything would go completely blank. These were lyrics I had played and sung over and over again for decades. It was a very different sensation than saying: 'Oh, it's on the tip of my tongue.' Everything was wiped clean. I kept thinking of *No Exit* by Sartre. Trapped in nothing. A wide expanse of nothingness. It was absolutely terrifying."

For Pollentier, one single, existential question remained: How would she make sense of her world?

———— ∞ ————

From a Silicon Valley perspective, the answer to Pollentier's question can be found in the natural sciences. Their theory for how the mind works is called "computational theory of the mind," or the idea that the brain works like a computer encoded in numerical renderings of zeros and ones. The head of engineering at Google, Ray Kurzweil, is one of the leading proponents of this idea, and his 2012 book *How to Create a Mind* describes how our soul and mind are mechanistic parts of the great computer of our brain. His thesis is called pattern recognition theory of mind, or PRTM, which characterizes our neocortex as a basic algorithmic function. He argues that we are already using engineering processes to deconstruct and augment the parts of our brain responsible for perception, memory, and critical thinking.

In this scenario, Pollentier's dilemma is less an existential reckoning and more a crisis of processing power and diagnostics. According to scientists like Kurzweil, her brain could soon be taken apart and analyzed in discrete bits. When she described feeling "empty" at the loss of her memory of song lyrics, for example, Kurzweil might comfort her with the promise of "uploading" these song lyrics back into her brain through a mechanism similar in function to a USB port.

Pollentier's actual recovery, however, looked nothing like Ray Kurzweil's vision of an algorithmic mind. Many months after her fall, she started to leave her apartment again to run errands and visit with friends. She took a part-time job working at a museum. And, eventually, Pollentier felt a longing to write poetry again. But she had no idea *how*.

Then, on a cool day last winter, she woke up with a surprising craving for tamales. To even experience a craving for food at all was unusual because the various medications and her constant pain left her stomach queasy. But something about the weather—the crispness of the sun and the slight bite in the air—triggered a sensation in her. It was "tamale day."

Without being fully aware of her own intentions, Pollentier described how she wandered into her small kitchen. She began to season her cast iron skillet and, from the experience of that action, she said she had the most intense and curious impulse. She grabbed a pencil and wrote something down on a scrap of paper.

"It was the combination of all those things: the skillet, the feeling of the day, the smell of the olive oil and chili peppers. I could feel it getting stored in my brain's waiting room differently. I thought, 'Oh I am definitely tucking this away.' And at that moment—as I was putting pencil to the napkin—I suddenly became acutely aware of one thing: I was writing a poem."

For years, Pollentier had made tamales on Christmas Day, and this day felt like a Christmas kind of day. It was early winter. It was cool outside and the sun was low in the sky. It was within this particular context that she suddenly remembered how to make tamales. This memory had nothing to do with following a recipe or the idea of an ideal meal. Instead, its return had everything to do with moving back and forth in the space of the small kitchen and the touch and perception of the particular textures of mashed corn and spices and oils and a piping-hot skillet. While the tamales were cooling in a covered basket, she went back to her scrap of paper and finished her new poem—the first one since the brain injury over three years ago. She called it "building pathways in the neuroplastic city."

. . . I forget how to remember
the words that are like words
that are like other words
with uses that are different
or are houses to shadows
that suggest other things

and then it all comes back to me

What does it mean when a skilled poet starts again from scratch? A Silicon Valley scenario of Pollentier's journey might look something like this: "I am going to write a poem today. Should I begin with a poem about the idea of the tree out the window? I will take out a pencil, sit down at my desk, and then write it down, word by word. What is a sestina? What is a line break? Yes. There it is. And now—at last—the idea of a tree is captured on paper."

But the reemergence of her skills looked nothing at all like that. When Pollentier regained access to her knowledge of cooking and poetry, the skills didn't come back to her in incremental steps or discrete tasks. Despite what the computational theory of mind would have us believe, Pollentier's brain did not process one input or calculation at a time. On that winter day, the entire structure of cooking and writing returned to her in tandem with a myriad of detailed senses, textures, and nuances. Her brain revealed itself, instead, to be a dense web of worlds with overlapping meanings and skills. Ray Kurzweil would like us to analyze our souls, our spirits, and our love of art as pure biological processes in the brain. But the natural sciences will never adequately explain how Nicole Pollentier recovered her ability to write poetry simply by making a tamale.

Cultural Engagement and the Stages of Mastery

Most of us will never suffer from a traumatic brain injury. Some of us may not relate to the loss—and then the recovery—of an artistic talent like poetry. Very few of us will ever be so uniquely positioned to understand our own cognitive abilities and how they might be challenged. In all these ways, Pollentier is on an extraordinary journey toward healing her brain.

In one particular way, however, Nicole Pollentier's story should resonate with all of us. Contrary to the theory of mind that dominates the Silicon Valley culture, her case shows us how we learn, think, and live in worlds. Using a kitchen knife is meaningless without everything else significant in the world of cooking: ingredients, plates, guests, and so forth. Poetry is impossible for Pollentier without muscle memories of the worlds she is attempting to describe. When she reaches out for the olive oil to her left and the scrap of paper to her right, her actions are summoned from deep within her by the social context.

In his book *Mind Over Machine*, Hubert Dreyfus, the preeminent interpreter of Heidegger and professor of philosophy at the University of California, Berkeley, outlines a phenomenology of skill that directly challenges computational theory of mind. His interpretation provides some insight into Pollentier's recovery and its implications. Dreyfus argues that human learning and skill cannot be reduced to rational calculations according to set formulas. Instead, he maintains that, as people learn a new skill, they progress through a series of phases of mastery. Early stages are defined by the application of learned computational rules and rational calculation, but later stages are characterized by a finely honed intuition that works below the level of our awareness. This intuition begins to draw parallels between unexpected patterns and, ultimately, to reinvent all the rules once considered sacrosanct.

Dreyfus's ideas, developed in collaboration with his brother, provide a framework for understanding how experts achieve mastery through an engagement with culture and social context. Just as Pollentier can only ever write poetry when she can access the *world* of poetry, the masters I introduce later in the book become most effective once they have fully immersed themselves in the world of their chosen endeavors. This is how human intelligence works, and it is a marvel of sophistication. Dreyfus breaks down how such a progression happens. Here is my summary of his five-stage process:

Stage 1: Novice. In the first stage of skill acquisition, the novice acquires rules for determining actions based on "context-free" elements of a situation. Dreyfus calls the manipulation of these elements according to prelearned rules "information processing." This is what happens when, for example, a beginning driver shifts gears in the car when he hits a certain speed regardless of whether he's going uphill or how fast the engine seems to be working—because he understands that he's supposed to shift at that speed. Or, to take another example, a novice business school student simply plugs in market share, sample survey results, and production costs into a cost-profit model to calculate a market analysis.

Stage 2: Advanced Beginner. The second-stage learner is able to recognize a pattern based on prior experience. These patterns are "situational" (in contrast to "context-free"). For example, a dog owner's recognition of his dog's distinctive bark, or the chess player's recognition of overextended positions. A beginning novice sommelier can take decontextualized elements, such as a wine's vintage, varietal, and region, and insert them into learned formulas to help determine if a particular bottle is "good" or not. However, these rules only take him so far—the rest of his judgment is based on his previous experience with wines from that year and region. The key difference between the first and second stages is that the advanced beginner learns to apply prior experience, rather than simply follow context-free prelearned formulas.

Stage 3: Competence. In the third stage, the number of context-free and situational elements is overwhelming, which forces the learner to adopt a hierarchical procedure for decision making that helps prioritize the most relevant elements of the situation. A competent head of sales, for example, will first determine if all of the sales goals are being met. If not, she will meet with each one of her sales teams and ask them why they are struggling with their numbers. When three of the four teams tell her that there are too many products in the line, she will initiate a conversation with her boss to winnow down the product list. During each decision in the hierarchy, she pays attention to only a few of the immense number of factors impinging on the overall project. She does not, for example, attempt to discern if there is a less rational reason for her team's struggles with their numbers. This type of behavior is a rational problem-solving process that makes use of both prior experience and computational rules for executing tasks.

Stage 4: Proficiency. A proficient learner engages in a rapid, fluid, and "involved" behavior that is not characterized by rational application of rules. Rather, it is characterized by recognition of patterns that emerge out of the accumulation of past experience. The proficient learner sees the situation in its totality, rather than as discrete elements whose relationship can be understood and acted upon based on rules. In William Gibson's 2003 novel *Pattern Recognition*, the protagonist Cayce Pollard has an immediate, intuitive, and physically negative reaction to derivative corporate logos. It is impossible for her to explain which components of the logos are off—it's the thing in its entirety that evokes a visceral response and determines the course of action.

Stage 5: Expertise. When someone acquires expertise, their level of involvement with their practice becomes so involved that little rational thought goes into the process. "An expert's skill has become so much a part of him that he need be no more aware of it than he is of his own body." At this highest level of competency, decision making is arational (that is, assessment of the situation lacks conscious analytic decomposition and recombination). This is "involved skilled behavior based on an accumulation of concrete experiences and the unconscious recognition of new situations as similar to whole remembered ones." Masterful novelist Colson Whitehead, for example, described the pattern recognition process involved in his 2016 book *The Underground Railroad*. He had a strong visceral response when he asked himself the question: "What if the Underground Railroad was a *real* railroad?" Using that as a launching conceit for the book, he relied on his expert intuition to weave in pop fabulist moments he remembered from his childhood. "My earliest immersion into the fantastic was probably reruns of *The Twilight Zone*," he told the *New York Times*. "Slave girl Cora emerging from the literal underground railroad and seeing a skyscraper: That's a quintessential *Twilight Zone* moment, where you take a step in the wrong direction and suddenly you're in a world a little off to the side."

When the extremely skilled are absorbed in their craft, the effect is uncanny. They have the ability of revealing their world—and opening up possibilities for new worlds—in thrilling ways. Take Bill Bradley, the famed Knicks player and later Rhodes scholar and presidential candidate, when he was really on his game: "The over-the-shoulder shot had no actual name," John McPhee wrote in his 1965 *New Yorker* essay profiling Bill Bradley. "He tossed it, without looking, over his head and into the basket. There was no need to look, he explained, because 'you develop a sense of where you are.'" The proper course of action is not determined by the actor; rather, it emerges directly from the totality of the situation. It is a bodily—not cerebral—and totally absorbing experience.

Such is the description of Judy Garland's 1961 Carnegie Hall performance, hailed by many as one of the single greatest performances in American show business history: "When she sings 'Come Rain or Come Shine' and she combusts onstage at the end of it, that's how I always wanted to be as an actor," Whoopi Goldberg told *Vanity Fair* in 2011. "That state of grace that she goes into at the end of that song, when she sounds like she's shaking like a branch that's being blown, and she's slightly off-key—just slightly. But it doesn't matter, because she's on fire." Witnesses to this level of mastery often describe an almost mystical experience—they get the impression that the activity flows not from the master, but rather through him.

While the above examples highlight mastery of elite, performative activities like music performance and competition in sports, a similar, if less dramatic, phenomenon occurs in people skilled at executing all manner of tasks: preschool teachers bringing order to a room of young children, doctors pulling together a variety of data points to arrive at an appropriate diagnosis, or a personal assistant choreographing the daily ebb and flow of their boss's busy life. In all of these examples, mastery is characterized by an intuitive flow—an involvement in a world—rather than a self-aware, computational process.

Think about jazz musicians who come together in a club to play music for the first time together. The younger musicians might play just as they would in their own practice rooms. They are insular; they play only in relation to themselves and their "idea" of a perfect piece of music. They are stuck in the rules. Experienced musicians—masters—know that they have to let all theories and presuppositions go the minute they come together. They arrive at the show with their thousands of hours of practice—technical expertise is always a given—but the minute they open the doors to the club, they start tuning in.

They feel the temperature of the room; they listen to see who is sounding aggressive and who might be playing with a bit of timidity; they hear the sounds of sirens on the street and they incorporate the "beep beep" like a repetitive motif in the piece. As Miles Davis put it, "Don't play what's there; play what's not there."

Sensemaking invites us to "play what's not there": to start seeking out space in between the rules. When we really want to achieve an insight, we have to dig into the context, immerse ourselves more fully in a world. In order to do that, however, first we have to look more closely at our relationship to data— both thick and thin. How do we "know" what we know? And what type of knowledge gives us the confidence to bet big on killer market hunches?

Chapter Four

Thick Data—Not Just Thin Data

This book is an essay in what is derogatorily called "literary economics," as opposed to mathematical economics, econometrics, or (embracing them both) the "new economic history."... A colleague has offered to provide a mathematical model to decorate the work. It might be useful to some readers, but not to me.

—Charles P. Kindleberger,
Manias, Panics and Crashes: A History of Financial Crises

The Story of the Three Traders

One day in early September 1992, three currency traders were sitting in the dingy offices of their hedge fund on Seventh Avenue in New York City. With duct tape on the carpet and a shabby conference table in the middle of the room, this unassuming space seemed an unlikely scene for the most monumental—and profitable—bet of the decade.

The three men were in the midst of discussion, running through their various data analytics. This trove of data, however, did not consist of spreadsheets, benchmarks, or numerical models. The financiers were, in fact, unraveling a dense little nugget of thick data that required an empathic understanding of both bruised pride and aspirations of autonomy. Specifically, they were parsing out the nuances of a sparring match between Helmut Schlesinger, head of the German federal bank, the Bundesbank, and Norman Lamont, the British finance minister.

In the wake of the Maastricht Treaty, signed earlier in the year, the most powerful central bankers in Europe were working toward the goal of creating one single European currency—the euro. But before reaching this goal, they had to resolve all sorts of political, economic, and cultural impediments. Most of these obstacles involved the role of Germany's central bank, the Bundesbank. Economists generally agreed that hyperinflation after World War I had left the Germans vulnerable to the Nazi regime. In the years following World War II, with the horrors of the Nazi era behind them, the main goal of Germany's central bank was to keep inflation rates low to avoid creating another opportunity for a destabilizing political movement.

After Maastricht, however, the bank had another potentially conflicting agenda: the Deutschmark would now be responsible for anchoring the new exchange rate mechanism for the rest of Europe. The 1990 reunification between East and West Germany caused inflationary pressure inside the country, so the Bundesbank raised interest rates, a move they had made many times in the past. The higher interest rates, however, alongside the recession and low interest rates in some of the other European countries like Great Britain and Italy, caused liquidity to move into the Deutschmark. The lower currencies, specifically the pound sterling and the lira, were trading at the very bottom band of the exchange rate mechanism as a result of the Bundesbank's monetary strategies. Suddenly, the sovereignty of Germany's central bank—its historic priority to make policy in the best interests of the German people—was at odds with the overall vision of a unified European market. Where would the chips fall? Would the Bundesbank ultimately choose its own anti-inflation policy or would it maintain alliances with the other countries in Europe—keeping the dream of a unified currency alive?

After a contentious series of meetings in late summer and early fall, Helmut Schlesinger was incensed by the perceived audaciousness of Norman Lamont, who, banging his fist on the table, demanded that the Bundesbank take action. Instead, Germany retreated behind a wall of thinly veiled disdain. Schlesinger announced at a public forum that he did not want to guarantee any action on interest rates. Later, he told an audience that he had little faith in the notion of fixed currencies between European central banks.

Back in New York, our three traders were paying close attention to the unfolding drama. Had Lamont pushed Schlesinger too far? Were Schlesinger's political ambitions with Europe, or with his own institution and the autonomy of Germany? How much stomach did the British government have for raising interest rates in the midst of their highly leveraged short-term mortgage economy? The head of the New York hedge fund—one of our three investors—had attended one of Schlesinger's conferences in Germany; the hedge funder immediately approached the central banker after the talk to get more nuanced intelligence. He asked Schlesinger if he agreed, in general, with the goal of a

European currency. The leader of the Bundesbank—a bureaucrat who had spent his entire career climbing the ranks at the central bank—replied that he did like the idea but that he was only interested in one name for that currency: the Deutschmark.

Despite the macroeconomic details, the plot points of this conflict might well have come from a reading list at a liberal arts university. Ego, political machinations, loyalty, wounded pride and ambition: these are the character traits you'll find in a great Shakespearean drama or a work of sweeping history by Thucydides.

One of the New York traders stood up to chart out a probability tree of the situation on a blackboard. It seemed more than plausible—given the characters and their circumstances—that the Bundesbank would choose its anti-inflationary policy over saving the other currencies and their devaluations, particularly those of Italy and Great Britain. With the economy already in recession, higher interest rates in Great Britain would immediately hurt the British people. In order to keep this new exchange rate afloat, the men decided that three things could adjust: German prices could go up; British prices could go down, or the exchange rate would adjust.

From these three scenarios, the traders walked through the consequences: The Germans were not going to tolerate inflation because of their history; the British economy could not tolerate deflation because of its short-term mortgage market. The conclusion seemed very clear: the exchange rate would have to adjust. The British sterling was almost certain to sink in value and the German bank would do nothing to save it. It was obvious to all three of them: the best speculative opportunity for them was shorting the British sterling. It was a no-brainer.

"What is the probability that the British bank will have to devalue in about three months?" one of the men asked.

"I'd say it's about 95 percent," the man at the blackboard answered.

The three men sat in silence for a moment. Within the boundaries of currency speculation, if they shorted the British sterling and they were wrong, over time they might lose a percentage of their position. But if they shorted the British sterling and they were right, they would make 15 to 20 percent off the position.

"95 percent on a 20–1 bet..." Their silence said it all.

Finally, the leader, the manager of the entire fund, asked his fellow investor, an expert in foreign currencies: "What would you bet on this one?"

The trader paused. "Three times capital?"

The whole of the hedge fund was currently valued at five billion dollars. Three times capital was fifteen billion dollars. If they took a position to short the British pound and they succeeded—that is, the currency did indeed devalue—they would surely bankrupt the entire bank of Britain and, in turn, disrupt the fundamentals of macroeconomic policy across all of Europe. The repercussions of their actions would be felt across the entire financial industry for decades to come and bring them under the scrutiny of financial regulators all over Western Europe. It would also make them both the most infamous and the most admired currency speculators in the world.

A moment later, the leader of the three calmly made his decision: "Let's do three times capital then."

And then he stood up and walked out of the room.

———— ∾ ————

Numerous investors made money on September 16, 1992, a day later dubbed "Black Wednesday," but no one made as much money as our lead financial speculator—George Soros—his heir apparent, Stanley Druckenmiller, and his then–chief strategist, Robert Johnson. Soros became known as the man who "broke the Bank of England." When the British government finally gave up and withdrew from the exchange rate mechanism— after weeks of attempting to buoy the sterling with artificially high interest rates—the British taxpayers lost $3.8 billion and George Soros's personal fortune was enlarged to the tune of $650 million. By some estimates, Soros Fund Management walked away with a profit from the trade of over one billion dollars. The head of Fiat in Italy claimed that it was more lucrative to be a a mere shareholder in Quantum Funds in 1992 than to own the entire enterprise of Fiat automobiles.

What happened in that room on Seventh Avenue? How did the three investors *know* that this was the moment for a big bet? Every serious financial firm in the world was looking at this chain of events. How did George Soros extract so much more data from the context than most other investors, taking into account not just what was officially said, but what wasn't said and why it wasn't said?

Soros arrived at this particular moment in time with a long history of engaging in humanities thinking. Decades before he was making world-famous speculative market calls, he was a student of philosophy at the London School of Economics in the late 1940s and early 1950s. His intellectual hero and mentor there was philosopher Karl Popper. While Soros studied under him, Popper indoctrinated Soros with an intellectual rigor based on his concept of "falsifiability," or the constant quest to prove how you're wrong, rather than prove how you're right.

As a philosopher of science, Popper's concept was concerned mainly with the cult of certainty that surrounded the scientific method: if you cannot find a situation in which the theory does not stick, then the theory holds. But no amount of testing, Popper emphasized, was exhaustive. "All the scientist can do, in my opinion," he wrote in his 1956 essay "Three Views Concerning Human Knowledge," "is to test his theories, and to eliminate all those that do not stand up to the most severe tests he can design."

Soros was originally captivated by these ideas as a philosophy student, but he soon learned that he could apply a version of "falsifiability" to great effect in market systems. He started to approach his market speculation with this same relentless drive to disprove his own sense of certainty about where the market was moving.

As a child who had grown up during an occupied Hungary in World War II, Popper's philosophical worldview also resonated with Soros's. "Where we believed that we were standing on firm and safe ground," Popper wrote in his essay "The Logic of the Social Sciences," "all things are, in truth, insecure and in a state of flux." Having seen the destabilizing forces of war throughout his earliest years, Soros was especially sensitive to the nonlinear movements of history. He recognized that sweeping events in politics were often a result of seemingly trivial personal snubs—the turf wars, indignation, and bruised egos simmering just below the surface of more rational monetary policy and treaties.

Stanley Druckenmiller and Robert Johnson were more traditionally trained economists—Druckenmiller left academia to begin a career as an oil analyst, and Johnson studied economics at MIT and completed his PhD at Princeton—but they both thrived under Soros's management style. The culture of humanities thinking at Soros Fund Management demanded that all three of them seek out the cultural context of their data.

Robert Johnson explained their unique process to me: "The data was not numbers mostly. It was not all quantifiable on spreadsheets. It was experiences, newspaper articles, stories about how people were reacting, conversations. Narrative data."

This is what I call *thick data*. What makes it *thick*? And why does it matter when machine learning gives us a surfeit of thin data? To answer these questions, I want to highlight four different kinds of knowledge, or ways of "knowing," that the field of philosophy helps illuminate. This will help us to recognize our bias toward thin data—or numbers stripped of their contextual meaning—and the ways in which that bias can keep us from uncovering cultural insights.

The Four Types of Knowledge

How do we know what we know? And how can we be certain we know something? Philosophers have pondered this question for millennia. Do I truly know that I am sitting on a chair, that $a^2 + b^2 = c^2$, or that Shakespeare is a great poet dealing with the topic of power? To people outside the world of philosophy, it seems absurd that such questions have created over two thousand years of debate. But philosophers really do spend much of their time wondering how we know that an object falls when we drop it or whether there really is a world when we close our eyes, and their insights should not be overlooked. Let's begin with the abstract ways of "knowing" that characterize thin data: objective knowledge.

1. Objective Knowledge

Objective knowledge is the basis for the natural sciences. "I know two plus two is four," "I know that this brick weighs three pounds," and "I know that water is made out of two hydrogen atoms and one oxygen atom." There is no real perspective involved in this kind of knowledge. This is why philosopher Thomas Nagel described it as "the view from nowhere" in his 1986 book of the same name. Objective knowledge can be tested and retested with the same results. Ants, atoms, and asteroids can all be observed and measured with objective knowledge because its claims are repeatable, universally valid, and correspond to observations in reality.

The proponents of objective knowledge have offered different frameworks over time, but we can trace its history back to positivism, the philosophical movement in the nineteenth century arguing that anything might be measured without the prejudice or value judgments of the observer. It's no coincidence that the nineteenth century—the height of the Industrial Revolution—was also the age of the machine. It was an era in which people were riding a wave of optimism based on the belief that science was rational and objective and that the human mind could conquer practically anything. In many ways it did: our advances in science modernized agriculture and transportation, made possible the transfer of goods across countries and across continents, and automated manufacturing processes to mass-produce goods that were needed for an increasingly wealthy middle class.

The idea that you could objectively measure and guarantee results fed into the production-oriented culture that was developing as companies became more focused on sharpening productivity and increasing margins. Alongside this fixation on objectivity, a new aesthetic of "realism" began to emerge. Theater artists strove to re-create entire cityscapes on the stage— life as it truly occurred, not as it we might wish it to—while writers like Zola and Flaubert focused on the objective reality of the "everyman" and "everywoman." Even the latter's poor Madame Bovary, a mere hausfrau with a hankering for romance, was worthy of a meticulously detailed examination.

Of course, those who know a bit about the trajectory of art and philosophy in the twentieth century recall that this certainty, objectivity, and rational thought were soon overtaken by doubt, subjectivity, and the irrational—in the form of dreams and the subconscious. The humanities moved away from the scientific "realism" of objective knowledge, as did many of our natural science fields: Einstein's theory of relativity, for example, was a major turning point in physics. Ironically enough, however, "management science" from the world of business continues to prioritize objective knowledge over all other types of knowing. This is why big data, with its ability to objectively measure quantities, outcomes, and iterations, is so appealing. It captures everything that occurs above the threshold of awareness: the clicks and choices and likes that characterize the reductionist versions of ourselves.

2. Subjective Knowledge

After objective knowledge, there is subjective knowledge: the world of personal opinions and feelings. It is the body of knowledge studied by cognitive psychologists, a reflection of our inner lives. We know certain things about ourselves that everyone around us respects as knowledge. When we say, "My neck hurts," or "I am hungry," people tend to defer to our own knowledge of our bodies and our selves. When a person experiences something belonging to the realm of the senses, it can only be accepted as true knowledge for them in that moment.

There are, however, surprisingly few examples of entirely subjective knowledge. When someone is at a ball game and they see everyone around them eating a hot dog, they are much more likely to say, "I am hungry." This is the type of knowledge that happens *in between* the subjective and the objective. It is knowledge about the world we share, and it characterizes much of what makes thick data so powerful.

3. Shared Knowledge

Unlike objective knowledge, this third form is not something that can be measured like atoms or distances. And, unlike subjective knowledge, this type of knowledge is public and cultural. It involves a sensitivity to our various social structures, or, to use the concept that I introduced in Chapter One, our "worlds."

Put another way, the third knowledge is the realm of shared human experience. In Chapter Four, we will look at how this type of experience can be analyzed using the study of phenomenology: What is the Jewish experience? What does it mean to be a working woman in America? What does it feel like to migrate to the city in a rapidly urbanizing China?

For Soros and his colleagues, the third knowledge was an integral part of their big bet. They "knew" the German experience and how it was made manifest in the monetary policy following World War II. They "knew" the feel on the streets in London and how strapped the Brits felt by increases in interest rates. This is not universal knowledge; it is necessarily situational. And it is not inner knowledge but rather a shared codex. It is the being and knowing that we experience together. They were following the main event—the devaluation of the pound—but the speculative opportunities existed in the secondary and tertiary waves of events that would then occur. How might investors react to the drama that would unfold? And how would scenarios of greed or fear play out after that—what would be the response to the response?

Understanding moods, a form of thick data, was an essential element in this analysis. Moods are bigger than we are: they can take over a room, a city, or a country. We say, "I am in an anxious mood," not "An anxious mood is in me." This is an important distinction, because moods are inherently social. There is nothing objective about a mood, nor is there anything entirely subjective about them. Moods capture the way we all feel together, or how the way one person feels can affect those around him or her. The Soros team used their nuanced sensitivity toward mood to analyze the waves of excitement and panic that followed certain market moves after Maastricht.

4. Sensory Knowledge

The three investors also stayed attuned to a fourth type of knowledge coming from the body. This fourth knowledge tells us something about how we navigate through a lower-level understanding of our world. We see this knowledge when experienced soldiers in Iraq describe "feeling" the booby traps in their bodies upon getting near to them. Veteran firefighters recall understanding the movements of a fire through a "sixth sense," and expert paramedics are seen grabbing for the defibrillator before any explicit signs of a cardiac arrest are visible.

Soros describes his own body as *inside* the market system. Like a surfer becoming one with the surfboard and, by extension, the movement of the ocean waves, he experiences market data as a kind of stream of consciousness, inextricably linked to his own perception. He asks his colleagues and employees where they experience their best calls—the neck, back, head, or stomach—and he is known for making major investment calls based on a pain in his back or a bad night's sleep. Another investor at his firm described respiratory infections as a valuable piece of soft data about possible over-leverage in a position. When he started coughing at meetings, Soros immediately asked him: "Is it time to take some risk off?"

Synthesizing Knowledge and Pattern Recognition

While you might scoff at any correlation between bodily sensations and market knowledge, the myth of Soros as a shaman speculator should not distract us from appreciating a far more analytically rigorous process in his work. George Soros and his team were able to make killer calls not because they relied solely on a back pain but because they artfully synthesized all *four* types of knowledge. Most important for sensemaking, they did not prioritize any one as more valid than another.

By extracting more knowledge from the given context—using benchmarks and modeling as mere guideposts—the three traders in 1992 had access to significantly more information. Since most investors base their decision-making on models of rational behavior and equilibrium, the Soros team could predict the actions of the rest of the market players. If you know your enemy's world—if you are empathically engaged in understanding their perspective—you can take advantage of them with great market calls.

Let's take a moment to discuss just how radically different the information-gathering process was with Soros and his group compared to a more traditional bank or investment firm. While the group around the table at Soros Fund Management was keenly attuned to all four types of knowledge—synthesizing a data point like the German national pride along with an understanding of the British stomach for severe austerity measures—the people employed at a bank like Goldman Sachs or Morgan Stanley would have been far more likely to be working with a mathematical model designed by a highly intelligent and impeccably educated mathematician or physicist. Such models have absolutely no use for an unquantifiable data point like Norman Lamont's sense of indignation. These models optimize only one type of knowledge—objective knowledge. They claim to take risk out of the system by mapping out various scenarios on a global scale with one core assumption underneath all the activity: markets are rational and will always—eventually—return to equilibrium. Risk and reward are balanced and therefore fair and predictable. In this optic, human actors are also always rational, with clear and preset goals.

It's worth considering that almost all of this modeling takes place on the highest floors of glass buildings in places like London, New York, and Frankfurt, far away from the real world. The data and the models become a sort of window into the world through which the financial firm's employees may well feel that they can understand the entire global economy. Because of the underlying assumptions about rational behavior and equilibrium, there is no real need to get out of the office. It is a clean world: clean offices, clean assumptions, and clean intentions. Millions of dollars are lost and gained every moment based on a body of knowledge that isn't situated in any real or concrete place in the world—knowledge that only refers back to its own mathematical beauty.

Now consider how Robert Johnson, Soros's main expert in currency trading, prepared for his role in "breaking the bank of England." In the fall of 1991, he could sense the growing pressures of German unification, which were only augmented by the collapse of the U.S.S.R. Everyone knew that the Maastricht Treaty was going to cause the already stressed European system to unravel in some way. Johnson had a long position of approximately two billion dollars on the stability of the Finnish currency (markka), but he had started to doubt that investment. Although he might have sat in his office in New York or Paris and run the numbers through additional models, he decided instead that the best way to discern the next move was to live out of a hotel in Helsinki for the winter.

"They like to drink in Finland, if you haven't heard," he told me, "so I went out with them every night to a place called Café Mozart. Everyone had a lot to drink and, over the course of the winter, I got to know these people quite well. One night, they all started telling me about their simulations. These people were preparing for devaluation of the markka. I could hear it in their voices."

The next day, Johnson walked into the Central Bank of Finland and told them that he wanted to get out of his two-billion-dollar position. They made the transaction at the Finnish Postal Bank so as not to alarm the markets and, at ten o'clock that morning, Johnson was out of his bet. He caught the next plane home to New York and upon arrival shorted—or switched his position—to bet *against* the Finnish currency. Only days later, the Finnish currency fell by about 18 percent. Johnson walked away with substantial gains while almost every other investor in that market took a huge hit.

"Everyone was walking up to me and saying: 'How did you see that? How did you know they were planning to let their currency go?'" Johnson told me. "I knew because I was there. I could feel it in the room when I talked to the Finnish people—not just the officials at the central bank, but when I talked to the financial investors and the trade guys and the labor union negotiators. I learned it from real conversations with real feelings, not from fundamental mechanical economics."

Johnson compared this type of thick data with the thin data considered "legitimate" at his alma mater, MIT: "When I took a mathematical formula from economics over to the engineering department and I put it in on the oscilloscope, it fit like a glove. When I applied it to labor markets, however, it never made any sense. 'What are you guys doing?' I said. 'You're pretending. These are human systems, not mechanical ones.'"

Johnson wistfully described his encounter at MIT with one of his mentors, famed economist and historian Charles Kindleberger: "This guy would invite us all to go the last rehearsal of the Boston Symphony on Friday mornings before the weekend performance. He would take us all out for coffee and a muffin and we'd go listen and then we'd have a sit around afterwards. This guy lived economic history: He worked on the Marshall Plan and he wrote the famous book *Manias, Crashes and Panics*. His pattern recognition came from circumstance, history, human stories. He told bankers that books by Defoe, Balzac, and Dickens were all important books for genuine sophistication in the field."

A Return to Literary Economics

Economics, as a discipline, is a perfect example of an activity that benefits most from all four types of knowledge—data thick *and* thin. Why, then, do so many insist that it should reside solely in the realm of objective knowledge? The great economist Paul Samuelson spoke to this conflict in an interview on PBS's *NewsHour* in the late nineties:

Economics is not an exact science, it's a combination of an art and elements of science. And that's almost the first and last lesson to be learned about economics: that, in my judgment, we are not converging toward exactitude, but we're improving our databases and our ways of reasoning about them.

Historian Isaiah Berlin had a unique insight into this particular kind of lesson. He spent much of his academic life studying politics, seeking out a description for political insight and leadership. During the period in which he was writing his books and essays—the mid-to-late twentieth century— political scientists and economists were fixated on finding the universal laws and frameworks for all political systems. They argued that these types of theoretical concepts could guide entire social and political bodies to move forward in the manner of scientific progress. They wanted politics to play a rational game.

Berlin set out to investigate these arguments in his 1996 essay collection *The Sense of Reality*. Was this rational game an accurate reflection of reality? Is this the way that politics actually played out? What he discovered, throughout his investigation, was quite the opposite. Much as a master investor like George Soros is able to simultaneously synthesize inputs of inconceivable complexity, Berlin found that great political leaders had a set of personal skills that he called *"perfectly ordinary, empirical, and quasi-aesthetic."* These skills were characterized by an engagement with reality founded on experience, empathic understanding of others, and sensitivity to the situation. It's the extraordinary ability to synthesize *"a vast amalgam of constantly changing, multicolored, evanescent, perpetually over-lapping data, too many, too swift, too intermingled to be caught and pinned down and labeled like so many individual butterflies."*

If we follow Berlin's argument, the gift of these investors is to be able to *see* patterns in a vast ocean of data, impressions, facts, experiences, opinions, and observations and to then connect these patterns into a single unifying insight. In his mind this requires a *"direct, almost sensuous contact with the relevant data,"* an *"acute sense of what fits with what, what springs from what, what leads to what."*

This skill combines reason, emotion, judgment, and analysis, or as Berlin put it: *"so many individual butterflies."* And, in the context of financial speculation, it also requires the nerve to *act* on all four types of knowledge.

Discipline and Action

On October 19, 1987, the Dow Jones Index lost 22.6 percent of its value, the biggest drop for the index since its incarnation in 1896. Market watchers were trying to read the signs in the precipitous drop of the day, soon dubbed "Black Monday." Druckenmiller thought he could discern a pattern familiar from previous crashes: based on experience and historical knowledge, he theorized that a sharp fall in the markets would be followed only days later by a rally and then a dramatic fall. Soros, on the other hand, read the market signals as a symptom of financial engineering. He was convinced that the newly developed financial product called portfolio insurance had produced a destabilizing feedback loop in the markets. The product was meant to protect investors against significant losses in the case of a market fall, but when thousands of investors purchased the product, it triggered a free-for-all in futures selling. Extreme movements in this seemingly small corner of the market—like the wings of a butterfly in Japan—ultimately created enormous market volatility.

Because Soros was convinced that Black Monday had been caused by these complex feedback loops and not from a fundamental shift in the market bottoming out after the bubble, he kept his position and remained bullish. On Wednesday, October 21, however, Soros watched his bet to short the Japanese yen fall flat as the market in Tokyo was starting to rise. He realized that the U.S. market was, in fact, bottoming out and that the oscillations caused by portfolio insurance were only a small part of a bigger bust cycle. His fund was hemorrhaging money and he would soon lose credibility with his investors. Only weeks before, his Quantum Fund had been up 60 percent for the year, and now it was down 10 percent. Soros got out of his positions in a fire sale so large it shifted the entire movement of the market. In a matter of days, $840 million from his fund went up in smoke.

He was not alone. Storied hedge fund managers were taken down right and left as the market made a mad dash for the bottom. Soon after the crash, Soros attended a party with several prominent investors. Unsurprisingly the atmosphere in the room was morose. Billionaire investors—once masters of the universe—were despondent over their inability to predict market volatility. Legendary hedge fund manager Michael Steinhardt greeted guests while lying in the fetal position. He told colleagues that he was ready for a career and lifestyle change.

Soros was keenly aware of the mood of the hour—and the

markets—but he did not allow himself to succumb to them. He used his intellectual acumen to act in the midst of the funereal atmosphere. He could see that Alan Greenspan, then-head of the Federal Reserve, would ease credit massively to allow for more market movement. While most shaken investors remained in recovery mode that week, Soros never lost his nerve. He made a swift move shorting the dollar in the Foreign Exchange Market. It was a position of pure bravado, another bet on other people's bets just days after the losses of Black Monday. But, he later described, his mouth literally watered "like one of Pavlov's dogs" at the speculative opportunity. As anticipated, the dollar fell and his move was a success. By the end of 1987, Quantum was up again, this time by 13 percent.

Most of the other investors at that party in 1987 had access to the exact same information and economic models as George Soros. Everyone knew that the Federal Reserve would ease monetary policy to avoid a complete shutdown of the market. If you had asked any one of the power players—whether in the fetal position or drowning their sorrows in a drink—they would have predicted the exact same series of events. The difference is that Soros had cultivated a disciplined mode of practice: he was able to remain dispassionate toward his recent losses because he was focused on the new speculative opportunity. By removing himself and his wounded ego from the context, he only felt what the market felt. And that feeling was one of tremendous opportunity.

Soros trained himself to rigorously stay open to all types of knowing. In using his body and the cultural context, he kept himself from growing too attached to the objective knowledge of the numbers: "Confidence is not a choice, but what George

Soros does is a choice," Johnson told me. "It's his underlying belief in his ability and the choice he makes to *act* on that ability. That's what I marvel at: his ability to act. It's not that he can logically recognize the most lucrative actions to take; many highly skilled people in our field can do that. It's the fact that he actually takes the action. He doesn't stand aside from the battle to observe. He acts from inside it."

From the Atmosphere to the Stratosphere

Chris Canavan, who has a PhD in economics from Columbia University and currently works with Soros, differentiated his own tendencies from those of his boss: "When I was a trader, like Soros, I remember having hunches or an inchoate sense of how a market might move or would move. And in retrospect, I would realize that I was right and I was responding to something that was going on around me. But I wasn't willing to listen to it; I wasn't willing to allow it to alter what I was thinking. And I say 'thinking' in a kind of empirical way. You have the skill to intuit that you're at an inflection point and you may even have a sense about which way something is going to break, but I was still too timid to take advantage of that information or knowledge, because I couldn't express it numerically. And few of us have the ability to tell others around us that we're betting on a position not because the numbers are telling us to do so but because we just *know* it's the right thing to do."

Canavan likens it to the mastery he witnessed as a young golfer immersed in the game. "The better I got at golf," he told me, "the more I began to appreciate just how truly great the great golfers really were." He explained the startling perception shift he experienced in the presence of golf masters. Though he was moving closer to the elite athletes in terms of his skill level, his advancement only showed him how truly far ahead they were in their understanding of the game.

"They achieved this exponential lift-off and they moved into a stratosphere. But unless you were a good enough golfer, you didn't really appreciate that they were in a stratosphere and not just the atmosphere."

This "lift-off" was only made possible through the courage to act on *all* types of knowledge. "An average player," Canavan explained, "just doesn't realize how complicated it is to factor in all of these variables—wind, temperature, the grain of the grass, all of this—and then decide how to hit a shot. But, perhaps most important of all, to have the courage to hit that shot knowing how narrow your margin of error is."

Not all of us can personally relate to mastery in golf or, say, jazz piano, but most of us have seen mastery at work in the way we acquire knowledge of a new language. The newcomer to German will need to start with learning the rules of the language, or the grammar. The student is concerned with questions like, *How is this language organized? What are the rules, and what are the exceptions to the rules?* After some time immersed in the vocabulary, the student begins stringing sentences together, working diligently to avoid mistakes of grammar. Soon enough, the assiduous student becomes accustomed to rules like always putting the verb at the end of those (very long) German sentences. And then, just as Canavan described, the student leaves the atmosphere and zooms into the stratosphere. Like magic, she lets go of all thought and relaxes into fluency. The rules themselves—those principles of abstraction—withdraw and she speaks in the new language with a kind of fluidity and porousness: she bends the language to her will, plays with it, owns it as a tool of expression. The experience of searching for a vocabulary word is now entirely in the background, and a focus on the meaning of what she wants to say is front and center of her attention.

In this example of mastery, as in so many others I will turn to throughout the book, we can refer, again, to philosopher Hubert Dreyfus. For Dreyfus, and for other philosophers working in the phenomenological tradition, our greatest skills and innovations are not the result of conscious thought. Though this seems obvious when we discuss acquiring a new language, it is actually in radical contradiction to the prevailing norms in many corporations, institutions, and even education systems that explicitly and tacitly assert that our greatest skills are exhibited when we are sitting alone thinking abstract thoughts.

The Power of Practical Wisdom

Aristotle's notion of *phronesis*—or practical wisdom—helps us understand this better. He argued that the man of practical wisdom is able to transcend the "grammar" of the field in which he works. He no longer needs the training wheels of rules or models; instead he reads the context as *concrete* and *situated*. He does the appropriate thing in the appropriate way at the appropriate moment. When Canavan describes a master golfer, he is really describing the concrete reaction of a player to a specific situation. We might even say that his context *pulled* the action out of him. And, because he was a master, he was skilled enough to stay receptive to the meaning of the moment.

As Canavan put it, "The more you become a slave to this Cartesian way of thinking, the less willing you are to listen to your hunches and your neck aches and your upset stomachs. And that is going to make you a less successful, not more successful, trader or speculator. We operate with this paradox: the prevailing narrative is that the more scientific the information the better, and yet it shuts us off to all sorts of information that comes in a different form. But it's the people who don't shut themselves off to that information who, many times, outperform the others. And outperforming very often means it's a zero-sum game: my gain is your loss."

A senior trader I spoke with at the Soros Fund described his own experience of pulling from all four data streams. The trader was an extremely skilled advisor to the Brazilian government as well as a decades-long veteran in the South American markets. He used both of these experiences to take a risky leveraged position on Brazil in 2001. Things were looking good for him in the first quarter, but then his position started to lose money. And then it lost a lot of money. After six months had passed and several hundred million dollars had been lost, Soros called the trader up on the phone and asked him to stop by.

"My first thought was, well, I've had a good run and at least now I can say that I used to work for George Soros," he told me, laughing.

But when he met with Soros in person and tried to explain his reasoning for the disastrous position, something altogether different occurred. Soros stopped him mid-explanation after only fifteen seconds. He told the trader that he should keep his position; he said, "Wait until it can't get any worse, and at that moment, double your position." He was relieved but also flabbergasted at this directive from Soros. How was he to "know" when it couldn't get any worse?

He waited and watched the markets. Two weeks later, the trader looked at his position and there it was: he was filled with a certain understanding that the market really had bottomed out. At that moment, he turned back to the advice given to him by George Soros. At the very bottom of the market, when everyone was running from the position, this trader took a long breath and doubled down. He waited.

Consider for a moment how hard it was for a trader to double down and wait in the midst of the herd mentality to escape. Everything in his being was screaming out in panic: "Get out *now*." Instead, however, he used discipline to stay calm. He attempted to detach his own emotions from his involvement with his position.

And then, almost like magic, the market turned. No one was surprised by the fact that the markets turned: what goes down must eventually go up. What was shocking, however, was the way the market turned immediately after his experience of hitting the bottom.

"My years of looking at the markets taught me how to recognize it," he told me. "But George Soros was the one who showed me how to make big bets against the grain on that feeling. Our bet wasn't based on analytics but on the years and years of seeing the patterns in the market. This was something I could never codify or even explain really. But we got back what we lost several times over."

Chris Canavan described to me his most profound encounter with these alternative ways of knowing, or soft data. In 1997, he left his academic career behind and landed at Goldman

Sachs, where we often spent time on the commodities trading floor. It was there that he started to puzzle over some of the truths of his world: the average commodities traders—traders in goods like gold, oil, natural gas, and palladium, for example—were generally about three to five years older than the traders on the foreign exchange floor. The commodities traders were also generally perceived to be less intelligent than the foreign exchange traders. They didn't have the same pedigrees: the Ivy League schools, the prestigious internships. And yet, it was also well known that the commodities trading unit was a veritable powerhouse at Goldman; it had been one of the most profitable commodities businesses in the field for decades. Why were these guys, objectively not the smartest guys in the room, systematically landing the better trades?

Then one summer, a hurricane ravaged the Gulf Coast and headed inland toward Louisiana. Canavan watched as the commodities market went haywire. And yet, in the midst of this incredible volatility, he noted that the commodities traders were not just continuing to trade, they were trading at their best.

"These were guys who had been doing nothing but trading crude oil or refined products—stuff going into and out of a refinery—for the last twenty years," Canavan told me. "And they were in their element because they could summon up relevant information—without even looking any of it up—about all of the rigs along the path of the hurricane. But not only that, they knew which refineries along the Gulf coast and the Atlantic coast those rigs supplied."

Canavan realized that none of the traders were working from mathematical models. They weren't numerates searching for the best equation to objectively make sense of the market activity. Instead, they were completely immersed in the movements of the markets.

"They would say, 'Because I know where everything is and where everything is flowing, I can picture in my mind what is about to happen because I can just see the hurricane and its consequences unfolding. From there, I can map out the consequences that will give me a sense of which way the prices of crude and other kinds of products will move. And then I can take advantage of those anticipated moves by trading them.'"

During that period, he watched as the commodities traders made a profit throughout one of the most volatile periods of the decade. The traders on the foreign exchange desks, on the other hand, fared quite differently in the midst of instability.

"The general idea was to teach a sharp twenty-three-year-old college graduate a few basic mathematical concepts about how foreign exchange rates get set—or at least how we assume that they get set—and to give them some powerful models to compute these things pretty quickly. That person can start trading and make some money without having to accumulate bespoke and difficult-to-quantify information because of the nature of the market.

"I used to think: these young whippersnappers will take down the crude oil traders any day of the week." After the hurricane, however, he changed his mind about almost everything he thought he knew.

"Up until that moment, I believed the orthodoxy. Here I was: I had a PhD in economics and I had been in academia for a while. I thought a good trader needed to find a better model than the next guy. And I thought all of the work was in inventing and improving and refining the next sophisticated statistical technique to make that better model.

"After that hurricane, I realized that all the skills of this kind of foreign exchange trader get frozen the minute something unexpected occurs. I thought, 'I have to completely invert my sense of what a good trader is.'

"Someday soon we will approach a point where all quantifiable information will be processed by all market participants simultaneously and instantaneously. All that requires is faster fiber optic cable, more memory, and models. These models are proprietary for a day and a half and then everyone else has them. At that point, what distinguishes a systematically good trader from a systematically bad trader?"

The Cartesian prediction—based entirely on a rational market—is that all traders will begin flipping coins, no one any better than another. Canavan's prediction is different. He feels that, even in the midst of utter transparency, some traders will still be better. And some will achieve extraordinary results over and over again. These will be the ones working from real life— pulling and synthesizing data thick *and* thin. They will draw insights from understandings of *culture,* firmly grounded in the reality of each and every situation. After all, human intelligence at its best is never just a flip of the coin.

In the next chapter, we'll look at where we can access the type of thick data that matters most. Cultural study requires a methodology that acknowledges the complexities of our world. It's time to turn away from the promises of false abstractions and immerse ourselves fully in the richness of reality. We'll start with the study of an apricot cocktail.

Chapter Five

The Savannah—Not the Zoo

Philosophers, as things now stand, are all too fond of offering criticism from on high instead of studying and understanding things from within.

—*Edmund Husserl*

Husserl, Heidegger, and the Story of the Apricot Cocktail

Legend has it that Jean-Paul Sartre, Simone de Beauvoir, and their friend and colleague Raymond Aron were having drinks one day in 1933 at a café on rue Montparnasse. Raymond Aron had just come from Germany, where he had heard a lecture by the philosopher Edmund Husserl. The German philosopher, Aron explained to his friends, was looking for a way to bring the everyday richness of life back into philosophical discourse. His concept, phenomenology, was about stripping away the abstractions of intellectual discourse from objects and experiences. Husserl exhorted his students to always return their attention back "to the thing itself." Sartre and Beauvoir immediately leaned in to learn more. Aron picked up the apricot cocktail sitting on their table and told them that phenomenology was the philosophy of something as ordinary as a cocktail. Rather than getting caught up in the categories of the mind and the role of "thinking" in existence, this new philosophy was a description of how phenomena are experienced by us in our everyday lives. Husserl encouraged his students to place what he called "brackets" around the prevailing philosophy of the day—concerns about whether or not the apricot cocktail actually existed in reality—in an effort to focus on objects as they actually appear to us.

At this point in our journey, some of you may be impatient to learn the answer to a burning fundamental question: What does sensemaking look like in its everyday application? And, the corollary question: How can I develop a personal sensemaking practice? Where does it all begin?

Not all of us can be like George Soros. And it goes without saying that sensemaking is not a "seven secrets" plan for success. Instead, my goal is to open your mind to what it takes to lay the groundwork for more astute cultural insights. There is, in fact, a tangible method that provides an organizing framework for the sensemaking tenets we have discussed so far. This method is called *phenomenology*, or "the science of phenomena." Although the word rarely comes up in casual conversation (admittedly, it doesn't roll off the tongue), the concept is the philosophical inspiration behind sensemaking.

What *is* a glass of wine, for example? More than one hundred years ago in Germany, Husserl, the philosopher who so intrigued Sartre, began posing seemingly basic questions like this. He argued that we must describe the wine as it presents itself to our sensory experience and not get too caught up in a philosophical hornet's nest about whether or not the wine is "real." In Husserl's classes—what one of his mentees dubbed "phenomenological kindergarten"—his students learned to describe all manner of everyday life experiences: a concerto, a thunderstorm, an illness. This job of description was not haphazard, however. It was a rigorous attempt to strip objects of abstract theories or habitual assumptions. It was the phenomenologist's job to describe things as they actually appear and not as we think they should or could appear.

His work was fresh and exciting and he attracted many followers to his lectures in the German university town of Freiburg. Eventually, in Paris, Sartre and Beauvoir would go on to meld Husserl's early notions of phenomenology with their own unique French sensibility, and thus the existentialism movement was born.

Husserl's most famous student, however, was Martin Heidegger. Heidegger took the work of his mentor and turned it on its head by suggesting that even the most rigorous phenomenology was still in the tradition of Descartes. In other words, it was still about an individual sitting and thinking apart from any social context.

Heidegger set out to describe the phenomenon of *being* itself, or our shared existence in the world. Husserl's phenomenology focused on the meaning of the apricot cocktail as an *idea* coming out of Raymond Aron's head. Heidegger's radical new philosophy argued that the world is not characterized by the set of ideas individuals have in their heads. In fact, he concluded, there is nothing *inner* about our experience. His form of phenomenology directed practitioners to focus on the social structures of worlds. The cocktail, he argued, was only one piece of equipment in the underlying structure of café culture and the people inside it: the waiters, the people at tables, the bartenders. And everything in this particular world—the invisible background practices in each and every café in Paris—was a reflection of the French culture. If one wants to have any understanding of the French sensibility, the first place one should go is to the Parisian café.

Escape from the Zoo

I offer up these ideas to give you an intellectual context for phenomenology. For your own sensemaking practice, however, the most important thing to remember about phenomenology is that it calls us to return to the real world. Go back "to the thing itself." Instead of watching the lions eating food from a bowl in a cage, go out and observe them hunting on the savannah. Escape the zoo.

Most of us are confined in our own kind of zoo. It is the airless office with glass windows high atop the bustling city. Or the conference room table covered in numerical representations of life. Or maybe it's the corporate strategy session with its empty mantras and meaningless acronyms. Whatever our zoo, it typically keeps us from capturing real life in all its complexity.

Phenomenology will not reveal the essence of something—say, a car or a restaurant—but rather the essence of *our relationship* to that thing. Not everything is important to us all the time. We stand in relationship to the things in our life, and phenomenology can show us which things matter most and when. In a pharmaceutical company, spreadsheets can tell you how many salespeople met their quarter goals in 2016, but phenomenology will shed light on what, exactly, makes a good salesperson. In a Fortune 500 coffee company, management science can tell us how much "premium" coffee—priced at two dollars or more a cup—the average American drinks in a day, but phenomenology will help us to understand what constitutes the experience of really good coffee. In a fashion company, market segmentation models can illustrate how, exactly, different luxury consumers spend their money, but phenomenology will reveal the experience they are seeking when they do.

Another way to consider the difference between the zoo and the savannah is through the terms "correct" and "true." The criterion for a natural science explanation is whether or not it is correct. Does a claim correspond to observable facts? This "correctness" is independent of subjective beliefs. But, as we've discussed, when it comes to our shared worlds, the notion of correctness doesn't reveal very much.

We can be correct in using biological sex: one is either a man or a woman. But being correct in this sense tells us very little about what it means to experience masculinity or femininity. What is it *like* to be a man or woman?

When we think in terms of human phenomena, we begin to reveal characteristics with real explanatory power. This is the kind of interpretation that makes people nod their heads in agreement and say, "That is *so* true." Such a truth is not a universal law—it won't apply to all quarks and all asteroids. But it will tell us something profound about a very specific time and place and population.

Any phenomenon or behavior—playing, partying, traveling, sports, investing, learning, entertainment, eating, beauty, or trust—can be analyzed using an interpretation that is "correct," or one that reveals "truth." But only via the latter kind of analysis does cultural meaning begin to manifest: a piece of fabric with three sewn colors becomes an American flag, a collection of molecules constituting gold becomes a wedding ring, and a structure made of plywood of varying lengths becomes a home.

Our experience in the world has to do with our investment in such objects and activities. Although the grapes might be exactly the same, a plastic cup of champagne at a loud party is a vastly different experience than receiving a champagne flute from a white-gloved waiter at a fine restaurant. Yes, it is correct that both may be made with grapes originating from the same field in France or that both contain identical milligrams of yeast, but one experience will leave you feeling sloppy and raucous, while the other can enchant and elevate you. The difference between the two experiences is where we find truth.

Consider the concept of time from a natural science perspective versus a phenomenological one. People say things like, "Oh, is it three o'clock already?" If you consult a clock, it is of course 3 PM at the same time every day. Through a natural science lens, time is fixed and decontextualized. A second is a second: like a string of matched pearls, each of the exact same size or duration. Looking back at your life, then, is like looking at an even set of units (minutes, years, decades) with the exact same properties. These are measurable and clear and, in principle, they can be exchanged for any other with the same outcome.

But this is not how time is *experienced*—not by a long shot. This natural science view of time is perfectly correct, but also perfectly superficial. In human or existential time, one second might feel longer than an hour. Waiting at the doctor's office is experienced as slower than running to the train—even if both events take the exact same number of units. Meaning is layered into the experience of time; the same time in your life can have different shades of meaning as you grow older. If you are in a gloomy mood as you consider your past, your twenties can look like a waste, while in an upbeat moment the time you spent in college might strike you as adventurous. Your past is dependent on the context you are in now and can change color based on the way you experience life now.

Such change is not limited to individual experience—it goes for shared cultural memories, too. The significance of a certain period or figure can change when new insights about that time and person come to light. Neville Chamberlain's decision to give certain portions of western Czechoslovakia to Nazi Germany in the 1938 Munich Agreement was seen as a savvy move to appease Hitler at the time. "Peace in our time," the crowds in Britain cried out upon his return. Today, however, we see things quite differently. Chamberlain is often viewed as the great coward of World War II: the man who fatally failed to stand up to evil. Needless to say, time changes the context in which we understand all historical events.

The same comparisons can be made for "space": think about the room or vehicle you are in right now. The natural sciences can describe the space based on the measurements you can plug into an algorithm. The distance between you and the wall, or you and the door, the height, temperature, and so on are all real and worth describing. But a phenomenologist looks at space in a very different way. The rooms you are in have a history, a mood, and a sense of place. The distance to the wall might be 6 feet, but is it *experienced* as far or close? We could spend decades assembling an exhaustive list of attributes of the Piazza Navona in Rome, but no list could ever come close to capturing its history of architecture and sculpture—created by the two great archrivals of Baroque Rome, Bernini and Borromini—and what it feels like to stand amid its splendor.

All great managers and CEOs use a kind of informal phenomenology when they are attempting a major overhaul to incentivize the best people. Politicians turn to a form of phenomenology when they strategize about how to turn a proposal into a bill with a chance of becoming law. And phenomenology is the first place to go when you are interested in engaging with a sensemaking practice. Whenever I am struggling to understand something involving culture and human behavior, I eventually reframe the problem as a phenomenon. I escape the zoo and I go out and observe life on the savannah.

What Is It Like to Age?

In 2015, my company partnered with the largest life insurance and annuity fund in Scandinavia. The firm was concerned because they were losing 10 percent of their customers every year. Even more troubling, most of the customers abandoning the company were older—around 55 years old. The business model of annuities is based on taking a percentage of the client's money over many decades in exchange for an amortized payout upon retirement. It follows, then, that the oldest customers are the most lucrative because they have the most money saved in the financial products.

When we started our work together, the client told us that annuities were a "low touch" product, meaning consumers were not in contact with them every day. They felt that annuities were only really present in people's minds twice in their lives: when they opened them up and when they were paid out. The company seemed resigned to the fact that their products were an uninteresting, albeit necessary, aspect of modern life. They were looking for a straightforward "inside the box" solution— perhaps a branding change—to help them turn their numbers around.

Our sensemaking process began with a discourse analysis of the client's own culture. *Discourse analysis,* based on social science theories inspired by Heidegger, examines how people and social communities give words and concepts meaning and significance. How did the culture inside our client's company conceive of annuities, pensions, and other financial products, and how was that communicated to their customers? Through this interrogation, two competing structures of reality were revealed:

1. The company culture was a part of the banking and financial world. In this context, logic and reason are paramount and the executives communicated with one another mainly using an assembly of acronyms. Customers were not called "people"; they were referred to as PSNs, or Personal Security Numbers. Considering this, it made sense that the executives were more sensitive to numerical representations of the PSNs than to the context of their products in real life. They spent their days looking at sales targets and percentage points with

combinations of letters like PSN and CMR instead of seeing actual people in relationship to their worlds.

2. The other reality sensemaking revealed was the way the client communicated to consumers through their marketing materials. Every pension and annuity product represented aging in the same way: there were pictures of gray-haired people on a bike or walking together down a beach. The mood and underlying message of the marketing was always about freedom. It was the Scandinavian version of "heaven": healthy, happy, stylishly gray-haired people enjoying life.

Ironically enough, this representation was just as alienating as the acronyms and financial figures. The assumptions behind all the marketing materials didn't resonate in truthful ways with the consumers. There was no authentic engagement with the reality of aging. No mention of the boredom and the increasing fatigue, no acknowledgement of the despondency and the loneliness. Real people know that getting old is not heaven on earth. It's a challenging experience. Why is a company that specializes in products for older people so distant from their actual reality?

Based on our understanding of the client's culture, we went to the CEO and told him that we wanted to do a study on aging. They were dubious, but we sat with the executives around the table—essentially a group of bankers—and asked them to leave the financial world altogether. We said: Let's talk about how we experience aging. Is aging a linear process? Is it connected to the number of years? How old is *old*?

Thus began a very rich conversation with the executive team. We agreed that we all experience aging in jumps rather than sequentially or linearly. *Now I am getting older, I probably need to spend more time with my kids.* Or *Now I am getting older, I probably need to pay out the mortgage on my house.* Or *I have to speak more kindly to my wife because we might not have ten years left.* Or *I probably need to slow down at work and do something else because I love art.*

And everyone around the table recalled moments when they were younger: pivotal moments when they had said, "I'm not a kid anymore. I am getting older." These moments changed their ways of dressing, what they ate, who they were with, how they built their social network, what they read. They changed everything. We said: do you think there is an interesting connection between discovering our aging and how it relates to finances?

And then we went to the whiteboard and drew up a map. We said: your problem is that you are losing customers. But you are convinced that your product is boring and that people don't care. What if we went out to study how people experience aging and what that *means* for understanding people's conceptions of a "good life" as they get older? If we understand that, then we can design pension and annuity products around that experience.

And that is when everyone around the table agreed to frame the problem as a phenomenon: *what is the experience of aging?*

Now we were ready to start the ethnographic research. This is where the thick data of sensemaking is gathered. We chose people in different life stages all over Scandinavia and we spent three days with them. This included interviews, photographs, videos, observations on everything in their worlds, engaging them in journal writing, and recording all of their financial activity with a mobile app.

Because we were interested in the social structures around a person, not just individuals, we did ethnographic research on everyone in the subjects' network. How is reality constructed? We talked to the wife or the husband, the friends, the colleagues, the employees, and the boss. We went with the subject to the bank and we sat with him or her while they did banking on their computer. We would call the pension company with him or her and record the call with the company.

With each of the subjects we studied, sensemaking is always seeking an understanding of the same thing: *What is it like to be this person? How do they experience their world?*

The minute we started talking to the subjects about aging—and not financial products like annuities—the conversations were filled with emotion. Far from being a "low touch" topic, we heard intimate stories about illness, risk, and the loss of parents and children. After sorting through all of our ethnographic data—the thick data of sensemaking—a remarkable pattern started to emerge: at around the age of 55, many of our subjects described feeling a loss of control over their lives. These were mostly middle-class people with children, but the experience was similar across all geographies. Some of them described the existential crisis of watching their kids move away: "Should we find a new meaning in life?" "Should we stay in this big house?" "Do I still love my husband?"

Others experienced the feeling of aging at work when it dawned on them that they would never again be promoted. "I am never going to be the boss," "My entire career now is just a matter of keeping up," and "The younger people below me are moving up faster and faster and I am only sliding down." People described being treated differently at the office—"He's just part of the old guard"—and on the streets—"Watch out for that older lady." One of our subjects told us that he got a letter from the life insurance company communicating that he was now 55 and it was time to think about how he wanted his annuity to be paid out. He had not heard from them in thirty years, so he couldn't even remember which company he was with. "It was not the letter," he told us. "It was the feeling that letter conveyed. I was no longer powerful in the workplace. And I was no longer in love with my wife and I no longer understood what life was about. That letter was a kick in my stomach. That letter told me: You. Are. Old."

Almost every one of our subjects in this age bracket had just completed a major reorganization of their finances. They sold their house, moved to a rental, bought a boat, or set up an inheritance for their children. And all of it was done with one calculation in mind: how long am I going to live?

By studying the phenomenon of aging, the company could see that these people were wide open for business. If a financial services company called them with the right question at the right time and framed the conversation the right way, these subjects were eager for advice. Not just about annuities, but about reorganizing their life. But these were the very customers that the firm was losing. Why?

While our client was ignoring these customers—assuming that by leaving them alone they would simply keep up the habit of saving for their annuity—other financial firms like banks were stepping in. They could see that this cohort was eager for advice on the whole financial picture and they started offering packages that included annuities alongside a whole bucket of other services.

Our client told us that 95 percent of their resources in customer sales went to acquisitions. This seems like an impressive percentage point when viewed through the management science lens. After reviewing it in context, however, we discovered that the majority of these sales efforts were directed at customers just starting their first jobs around the age of 22. The firm's 3,000-some annuities advisors were spending almost all of their time and resources on wooing these younger customers. If we know anything from studying the phenomenology of aging, it is that 22-year-olds cannot "see" death. The fact of death is irrefutable—again perfectly correct—but also perfectly irrelevant to 22-year-olds for whom parties and concerts and other fast-paced, vibrant activities take precedence. As a result, annuities held little meaning in their lives. When we analyzed the calendars of the sales force, we found that 70 percent of their meetings with potential twenty-something customers were canceled the day before. It was clearly a huge waste of resources to put in time and money trying to meet with customers who didn't want to meet to discuss an offering that they considered irrelevant. Meanwhile, the customers open and eager for business—the older customers—were being ignored in the hopes that sheer inertia would keep them from switching up their finances.

After the patterns became clear to the firm, the business recommendations evolved organically: digitize the interface for the young people so they don't have to take time to meet with anyone. And pour all of the time and money into the older clientele who are aging and eager to engage on the topic of financial planning.

After applying the business insights revealed by the sensemaking process, our client increased contributions to pensions and insurance premiums as well as the size of their customer engagement. Most importantly, they reduced their attrition rates—the number of older customers leaving—by 80 percent in the two years following the study. All of this was accomplished without increasing any costs in customer service.

As our client discovered, it makes great business sense to sit around and talk about the meaning of aging. What matters to your customers should matter to you.

Heidegger and Moods

What does it mean to be human? How do we experience ourselves in the world? Where does meaning come from? When we want to delve into questions this profound, the humanities are an extremely helpful guide. Most of us are probably not opening up great tomes of dense philosophical texts on any given Tuesday, but they can be an invaluable resource in the midst of reframing a problem as a phenomenon.

In the following passage, I will show you another example of phenomenology in practice. ReD recently drew upon Heidegger's definition of moods to help us reframe a business challenge involving supermarkets. In his major work *Being and Time*, Heidegger defines moods as not just cognitive or psychological phenomena but as things that "assail us" in our unreflecting devotion to the world. In bad moods, for example, we can see the world as burdensome, which will affect both what we might become engaged in and how that engagement will occur. Heidegger calls this mood-mentality *Befindlichkeit*, literally translated as "the state in which one may be found." In his view, moods are the phenomena through which humans get attuned to the different contexts they are thrown into. It follows, then, that a mood neither comes from the outside nor from the inside, but arises from our very existence in the world.

What does all of this have to do with the world of business—and, more specifically, increasing revenues in one of Europe's largest supermarket chains? As you will see, Heidegger's theories are far from esoteric. In fact, they formed the theoretical foundation of a major corporate reorganization.

How Do People Experience Cooking?

We recently partnered with a large European grocery store brand. Like so many of the large supermarket brands today—Walmart and Tesco, to name two—this brand was in trouble. Society has been changing in its attitudes toward grocery shopping, food, and cooking, and this brand—containing a variety of different types of stores under its corporate umbrella—was struggling to understand what was happening. The firm had 40 percent market share in their regions, but they could see that share beginning to slip. It was unlikely that they would capture additional market share, especially given the shifts in the culture. Instead, they wanted to try to increase the revenue per customer, encouraging people to buy more while in their stores. They had an idea that they could achieve this goal by promoting healthier, organic products. Beyond that hypothesis, however, they didn't really know where to begin.

Our sensemaking process started with an investigation of the supermarket's culture. What kinds of assumptions were underlying the company's structural understanding of the world? What does it mean to have a "supermarket-centric" point of view? The company had a tremendous amount of knowledge based on management science methodology. They knew what happened with customers when they were shopping in their stores. They knew all about revenue per visit based on sales prices, and the number of parking spots needed to reach capacity on a busy Sunday afternoon. They spoke fluently in price points and SKUs, or stock-keeping units: how many grocery items are contained in any given store. Arguably more important, the supermarket knew all about their "targeted segments." They could offer up abstract segmentation models for all different categories of shoppers: what women between the ages of 25 and 38 usually spent in the early evening visit, for example—the segment of working moms. They also knew exactly what size their aisles needed to be and the percentage of floor space they could dedicate to organic produce to optimize spending per visit.

All of this technical knowledge gave them a useful perspective, but a very limited one. They were experts in the domain of hard data about supermarkets. But what did they really know about their shoppers' *experience*? What did they know about what happened to all of that food as soon as shoppers arrived home? In the chain of meaning, the supermarket was only a means of achieving something bigger, something much richer and much more meaningful to people: *cooking.*

The client reframed the management science question— how do we increase the revenue per customer at all the stores in our brand architecture?—into a phenomenon: *How do people experience cooking?*

A generation ago, people tended to display their social currency through a big house or a fancy car or fashionable clothes.

Today, all of that is changing. Sophisticated urban dwellers have much less interest in these forms of ostentatious wealth. Instead, much of today's status—what sociologist Bourdieu referred to as "social capital"—comes from practices around food. People want to be able to talk about cooking; they want to name the local farm that raised their chickens; they want to know about methods of fermentation and baking bread; they want to be able to pair wine well with a meal.

Nowhere was this more evident than in sensemaking research with today's urban moms. Every single mom the company observed and interviewed for the supermarket project spoke of her dream of serving up fresh, healthy dinners to a family seated around the dinner table. And yet, the study took thousands of photographs of dinner tables across all the geographies it looked at, and every single one of them was covered with objects that were not related to eating. Most of them were used for the world of work—laptops and papers and bills and homework. Even more telling, the study couldn't find a single subject who could tell researchers what he or she planned to cook for dinner the next night. One grocery list we photographed captured this sense of unpredictability perfectly: it read "Grocery List: 1. Glue, 2. Soap, 3. Dinner."

Sensemaking confirmed what many of us already feel in our day-to-day lives: life and work are fluid. It is almost impossible to think about meals in any rational and linear way. Few people in urban areas come home from work every day at five o'clock and sit down to eat every night at six o'clock. Even fewer people plan out all their dinners ahead of time and shop for them in itemized lists.

Though none of these pressures on modern life come as a

surprise, the supermarket-centric view of the world was keeping this truth hidden from our client. There was an assumption in the supermarket's culture that shoppers came in with a single list for all their meals—onions, garlic, chicken—and that their primary decision was whether to conduct their grocery shopping in high-cost or low-cost stores. By focusing on phenomenology and the actual experience of families and how they cook, the client was able to see past all of these assumptions. People didn't shop in a conscious and predetermined way. They weren't "thinking" about it. Rather, they shopped intuitively, according to moods.

One of the moods sensemaking identified was the "evening rush." It wasn't just that one segment or another was shopping in a frenzy after work. *Everyone* in the study went grocery shopping in this mood. And a certain store experience delivers on this mood: It's five o'clock and the kids are hungry. We need to grab something fast for dinner and perhaps a few quick things for breakfast, too. In the evening rush, shoppers want a store that is easy to navigate and predictable, with quick and healthy dinner options readily apparent.

But evening rush isn't the only mood. Sensemaking uncovered another mood of inspiration: When guests are coming for dinner, grocery shoppers love spotting an employee acting as a chef and creating samples. They want to have exciting offerings showcased and new trends prominently displayed. They want change, dynamism, a curated selection, and a compelling narrative.

Using the work of anthropologist Clifford Geertz, sensemaking revealed that the supermarket was actually a kind of stage setting or scenography for the cultural narrative of cooking. Instead of a system of optimization—food as fuel—the supermarket needed to communicate different atmospheres in service of this theater. In the morning, the smell of fresh bread and coffee brewing entices shoppers, the music invigorates people on their way to work, and the lighting is bright and energizing. In the evening, however, the story shifts. People want savory smells and warm, dim light. Extra staff provide quicker checkouts. Cleaners come in before the evening rush so everything feels inviting and cozy; breakfast goods are whisked away and replaced with displays of fresh flowers to decorate the dinner table.

Once the store became a stage setting for the theater of food, new business ideas emerged. In an effort to make each store feel local and relevant, the client started to explore technology-enabled relationships between the store managers and regular customers. Imagine a busy mom with three kids in the car who receives a text message on her phone at 4:30 PM: "Hi, I'm Frank. I'm the store manager from your local market and I know you come here five times a week. We just got a batch of really wonderful salmon in from Canada. Would you like me to reserve one for you along with everything you need to complete our in-store recipe? I will have it ready for you to pick up at our drive-thru window."

In 2016, our client is using these sensemaking insights to open three pilot stores focused entirely around the concept of "evening rush," and they plan to open up forty more in 2017. They are also completely reorganizing their approach to digital technology with new loyalty programs and online food platforms. The biggest change in the company, however, is in their approach to shoppers' moods. Instead of segmenting their stores and brands using price point models like "high-end" and "low-end," they are now consolidating brands and closing down stores that target similar shopper moods. This strategic discussion around moods is leading the way the company positions itself in the market in 2017 and beyond.

It's not about measuring and tracking the number of purchases or the types of people who walk through the door. When we reframe the phenomenon as the experience of cooking rather than grocery shopping, we understand how decisions are shaped by the context we are in. Grocery stores can offer shoppers the experience they are seeking, regardless of segment or size.

These stories serve as an illustration of my own relationship to sensemaking and the way we use it within ReD Associates. Though the process is vastly different for everyone, all sensemaking requires its practitioners to bring something of themselves to the work. It is an engagement that demands every part of us—emotions, intellects, and spirits. Considering that, it is worth taking a moment to say a few words about *empathy* in its relationship to sensemaking.

When I say "empathy," I mean our emotional *and* intellectual skill of understanding another's worldview or cultural perspective. When we read a great play by Shakespeare or listen to a Beethoven symphony or sort through field notes in an anthropological study, we are not always familiar with the worlds we are encountering. This is why the empathy we use in sensemaking—what I will refer to as the third level of empathy—is different from the everyday empathy we experience for our friends or family. This third level of empathy requires a more analytical framework that is greatly aided by engagement with the realm of the humanities.

The Three Levels of Empathy

According to philosophers in the Heideggerian tradition, our most basic form of empathy—the first level of empathy—is below the threshold of our awareness. This is the kind of empathy we rarely ever talk about. We adjust to each other like Alice Munro's "spores"; we become more and more enmeshed in our immediate surroundings. As a non-native English speaker, I experience this type of empathic engagement with language. When I make mistakes—for instance, when I use a word in a wrong way or context—someone will often use that same word in the right way soon after to help acclimate me to the appropriate usage. I see this same empathic alignment in each and every company or organization I visit. There are always particular styles and codes that anyone entering the organization is socialized into. For example, in a fashion company I visited, employees were wearing black—a safe, basic wardrobe—but they chose pieces with signature details to communicate their edginess: not *too* safe. In marketing-driven organizations, on the other hand, the suits are more fitted and the language is more vague.

Some people say this first level of empathy speaks to our existence as social animals, while others call these shared worlds our "structures," or the norms and values through which we structure our reality. Sociologists and anthropologists have studied these structures for more than a century and debated whether they are fixed and eternal, or constantly changing.

What really matters for the purposes of our sensemaking journey is that this type of empathy is rarely ever noticed or remarked upon.

The second level of empathy is often triggered when we notice something is amiss. If a friend is exhibiting an unusual affect, such as sullen speech, we start to wonder what is going on with her. What is on her mind? Is she sad? Is it something we said? The intrigue over da Vinci's painting *Mona Lisa* is a famous example of this second level of empathy in action. What is she thinking behind that half smile? Is she feeling mischievous or circumspect? We can never quite synthesize the facial cues and the context. Try though we might, we feel we can never really get inside her head. First-level empathy moves up to second-level empathy.

If we want to engage in a process of understanding, we move to the third level of empathy, or *analytical empathy*. This deeper and more systematic empathy is supported by theory, frameworks, and an engagement with the humanities. This is sensemaking: the type of empathy Mark Fields uses to understand the next generation of Ford drivers. This is also what a historian does when she sets out to study, say, the American Civil War: She systematically assembles sources and evidence from that time—pictures, scrapbooks, tools, and news in order to get a picture of what happened. But the research materials are only the beginning. She will need to establish a context based on other scholars' work. She must also validate and critique the importance of the data, and place the data in a theoretical framework that explains the time period. The power structures, gender roles, aesthetics, technology, and information systems are all topics historians have created in order to analyze the data. Without this framework, her data would be merely reportage or journalism. Theory ultimately reveals the insights.

Fortunately for us, theories abound in the humanities and social sciences. There are frameworks for understanding everything from sexuality to family to power to social roles, to the role of art and music and stories in society. Once our thick data of ethnographic field notes, photographs, journals, and interviews is collected and sorted, our job is to identify the salient patterns occurring across all of the data. Good theory provides a structure for recognizing these patterns and, ultimately, one or two theories snap this raw data into focus. This is where we achieve insights with explanatory power: a more profound understanding of the phenomenon.

The following are just a few examples of what this process looks like in practice. These "sensemaking apps" offer a quick understanding of how the humanities and social science theories can be applied to real situations. After we have reframed a problem into a phenomenon, this process of analytical empathy brings us to a greater understanding of what we are encountering.

Six Sensemaking Apps

1. Signs and Symbols

THE THEORY:

Semiotics—the study of signs and symbols in social life— has always been a very important part of understanding human behavior. But symbols do not always represent the same thing to everyone, which is why researchers divide the symbol into two parts: the symbol itself and the *meaning* of the symbol. The correlation between the two is often random. A rose (the symbol) can signify love (the symbol's meaning) to one person and death to another. Individuals assign meaning to the symbol according to their personal backgrounds and situations.

THE THEORY IN PRACTICE:

An iconic French fashion company wanted to explore the types of symbols that illustrate success to today's high-end female fashion consumer. Our client was working with an assumption that their customers wanted to see images of women "having it all." These symbols showed women achieving career success alongside a family with children. Young children and glamorous careers were featured side by side in the lavishly produced commercials and short movies.

In a sensemaking study that observed these women in cities as varied as Hong Kong, L.A., Shanghai, Paris, New York City, New Delhi, and Chennai, we could see that these symbols of "having it all" were not resonating with consumers. Yes, they formed a part of the women's reality, but they did not fully explain why these particular women were engaged with and inspired by high-end fashion. Instead, the study revealed a completely different set of signs and symbols—many of them taken from the past and in reference to more "romantic" periods. These symbols—handwritten letters, silk dressing gowns, oyster shells, strings of pearls—were poetic and aesthetic. They communicated a desire for more enchantment in life. Fashion, for these women, was less about achieving life balance and much more about infusing modern life with moments of seduction and magic.

2. Mental Models

THE THEORY:

Political theorists Ernesto Laclau and Chantal Mouffe rooted their ideas of mental models around discourse theory. This is an analytical tool for examining the context in which words are used and the different ways they acquire their meaning. The word *freedom*, for example, can mean completely different things to different politicians. For a socialist, freedom means equal opportunity for everyone, with a close relationship to the idea of solidarity; while for the conservative, freedom means individuality, opportunities for the individual, and an association with inequality.

THE THEORY IN PRACTICE:

We worked with Coca-Cola to help them understand the market for bottled tea products in China. To the corporate culture of Coke, based in Atlanta in the southern United States, the word *tea* means a refreshing sweet drink that goes well with BBQ. For this culture, tea is all about additions: adding sugar and caffeine for a late-afternoon kick.

Through the theoretical lens of discourse analysis and mental models, however, Coke discovered that tea is about *subtractions* in the Chinese culture. Tea—like meditation—is a tool in Chinese culture for revealing the true self. The experience of it should take away irritants and distractions like noise, pollution, and stress. When Coke originally entered the market with their fruit-flavored sugar kicks, the Chinese culture didn't respond. It wasn't until Coke incorporated this fundamentally different understanding of the "tea experience" that their bottled tea products gained significant market share in China.

3. Niklas Luhmann's Theories around Social Systems

The Theory:

Niklas Luhmann, a German sociologist and one of the most important social theorists of the twentieth century, proposed that all professional cultures are built up around binary codes. For lawyers, it is important whether an action is legal or illegal. Economists are interested in whether the company earns a profit or not. Journalists want to know whether there is or isn't a story. These cultural codes are one of the reasons why professional worlds often misunderstand each other. Engineers think that designers are artistic and unsystematic, and designers think that engineers are rigid and introverted.

The Theory in Practice:

We partnered with a group that included health care workers and their managers. The managers, from their bureaucratic world, viewed success as achieving care "at-cost" as opposed to "not at-cost." The health care workers, on the other hand, were concerned with "good care" versus "bad care." The disconnect between these two binary codes explained much of the conflict that existed in the human system.

Before we could build any bridges between these two worlds, first we all had to understand and acknowledge the binary code of the culture—cost versus care—that was creating a fundamental misunderstanding.

4. Erving Goffman's Theories of Stage-Managed Impressions

THE THEORY:

In Erving Goffman's seminal study of cultural anthropology, *The Presentation of Self in Everyday Life* (1956), he outlined how individuals manage impressions in social interactions. He framed these interactions around theatrical encounters, naming the space in which we give our public performances the "front region," and the space where we knowingly contradict that performance the "back region." He argued that the success of performances in the front region depended on the privacy and respite of the back region.

THE THEORY IN PRACTICE:

In a sensemaking study with an appliance manufacturer, we noted two trends occurring in homes in North Texas and in the New York tri-state area. First, we found an increase in open-plan designs, with fewer walls and barriers and increasing flow between spaces in the house. At the same time, however, we observed an increase in investment in master bedroom suites and other private spaces, such as garages and pantries.

Drawing upon Erving Goffman's theories around public and private spaces in the theater of life, we were able to understand why these two trends were happening at the same time. As homes were becoming more public and accessible to visitors, people felt compelled to invest more in their private spaces. The appliances manufacturer, particularly interested in trends in laundry room spaces, was able to use this understanding to engage designers, architects, developers, and homeowners in a more meaningful way.

5. Theories of Reciprocity

The Theory:

In 1972, anthropologist Marshall Sahlins developed his three models of giving: negative reciprocity, balanced reciprocity, and generalized reciprocity. Sahlins defined negative reciprocity as a model in which people give in order to get more in return; balanced reciprocity as a model in which people give in order to get the same amount back; and generalized reciprocity as a model in which people give without any expectation of immediate payback because they trust that they will get more over time.

The Theory in Practice:

We worked with a major American museum to improve their membership program. They had large numbers of visitors and high interest, but they were struggling to transform these visitors into committed members. Even more important to the museum's funding, they wanted to convert visitors into donors at high levels of giving. Sahlins's theories of reciprocity—in particular his theory of generalized reciprocity—gave some clarity to the phenomenon.

A sensemaking study showed us that members viewed their relationship to the museum as primarily transactional. They often said, "Membership pays for itself," a view that was enforced by the way the museum rewarded its members with coupons and apparel. This transactional model did not foster a spirit of generosity. We worked with the client to shift their membership model from negative reciprocity into generalized reciprocity, or a reciprocity of trust. They encouraged members to think about giving to the museum as a gesture of altruism or an investment in a relationship to arts and culture. It also gave our client a strategic goal for their membership drive today and into the future: make membership an investment in a relationship, not a transaction.

6. Wittgenstein's Theories of Language

THE THEORY:

In his writing, Ludwig Wittgenstein argued that most of our language is not in words: the point is observation, not verbalization. When we see two mason workers building a brick wall, for example, almost everything they do is nonverbal. We won't understand anything about them if we fixate on their language. "Don't think, but look," Wittgenstein exhorted readers.

THE THEORY IN PRACTICE:

We worked on a study to investigate why people were burning the Danish embassies in the Arab world. It would have been easy to walk into the study holding tight to our own cultural ideas about what was occurring and to fixate on our understanding of the language around these events. For example, we might have quickly assumed that these were senseless acts of violence conducted by "Islamic terrorists."

Instead, we started with observation. We focused on the nonverbal communication that formed the structures of reality in the communities we visited in the Middle East. After immersion into the worlds of these communities, we started to see the frustration due to economic stagnation. Their belief in the Koran led them to believe that their society and culture would prosper and thrive. Instead, looking around, they saw only poverty and decline. The difference between these two visions formed the culture clash that was playing out all over the region—including in the embassy burnings.

Instead of rushing to the predetermined assumption first, we started with an attempt at understanding. This allowed us to suggest more effective choices later on in the process.

These examples of theory in practice serve as an illustration of how sensemaking actually works in real situations. Needless to say, the more one has empathically engaged with great books, art, theory, and music, the more one has to draw from in moments of pattern recognition. I have outlined just a few of the theories that have brought insights to the fore in my own work. Sensemaking, however, is ultimately an entirely personal practice. The more you dig into the vast wealth of art and theory available to you, the more you can crack mysteries at the heart of culture.

How do we remain open to these mysteries without getting seduced into solving them too soon? How do we reason through a problem involving human behavior that has no hypothesis and no clear knowns? This is the culmination of sensemaking: creativity that comes *through* us, as opposed to *from* us.

Chapter Six

Creativity—Not Manufacturing

Writing a novel is a terrible experience, during which the hair often falls out and the teeth decay. I'm always irritated by people who imply that writing fiction is an escape from reality. It is a plunge into reality and it's very shocking to the system.

—*Flannery O'Connor*
Mystery and Manners: Occasional Prose

Two Stories of Seeing

In 1910, a 23-year-old poet sat down to draft his response to the world around him. He channeled the voice of a middle-aged man straight from Dante's *Inferno*, circling round and round the increasingly empty rituals that made up his day. Like Shakespeare's Hamlet, his narrator was caught up in ambivalence, paralyzed by all action until the very act of consuming toast or drinking tea had become an existential crisis.

When I reread this poem—T. S. Eliot's "The Love Song of J. Alfred Prufrock"—a mood immediately sets in. I see the streets Prufrock walked in my mind; I wrestle with the ghosts in his head. "Shall I part my hair behind? Do I dare to eat a peach?" I *know* what it is like to live in a Europe on the cusp of modernity. This is a world where the gods have fled, a world without any divine glow of meaning surrounding human action. Prufrock's world is a place where even the most fundamental of cultural mores are being dismantled; all that is left is an endless and arbitrary assortment of empty rituals. As he says, "No! I am not Prince Hamlet": the existential question of "to be or not to be" is rendered irrelevant.

In 1914, only one year after Eliot completed this poem, the Archduke Franz Ferdinand was shot in Sarajevo, Austria-Hungary. As Eliot was putting his words down on paper, the world was beginning the process of remaking itself through war. Russia, Belgium, France, Great Britain, and Serbia were lining up against Austria-Hungary and Germany. Conflict was everywhere. The city of London—considered the most modern of all European cities—sets the stage for Prufrock's walk. He questions everything, even the very possibility of articulation:

It is impossible to say just what I mean!

The text of the poem itself serves as a portal to another world. Whereas Romantic writers before him endeavored to lose themselves in the idyll of nature, Eliot revealed an entirely new way of understanding poetry. In free verse and stream of consciousness, he undermines his own ability to even interpret his experience.

Eliot saw what others around him did not. He used fragmented structures, colloquialisms, and references to popular culture together with literary allusions from "high culture." He could sense that high and low were collapsing in on each other, that a new era was emerging. He gave voice to it. In many ways, he invented it. This is creativity at its most masterful: it is the act of opening up new worlds, of revealing entirely new ways of being in the world. Because of Eliot, our culture has an entirely different conception of the word *I* in a poem—and the word *I* in our everyday lives. This innovation alone makes him one of the greatest English-language poets of the twentieth century.

Across the ocean and a world away, a second young man was in the midst of articulating his own vision of the modern age. Unlike Eliot, however, this man's vision was filled with optimism. Born in 1863 to a community with a tradition of fiercely independent farmers and self-sufficient craftsmen, this man could sense a schism forming in the early twentieth century. As more and more members of his generation moved to the cities and took jobs in the rapidly growing factories or as white-collar workers in the bureaucracies of America's nascent corporations, the entire notion of "work" was being transformed. The typical day no longer involved waking with the dawn to do chores or following the seasonal demands of agricultural life. Nor did work demand the self-sufficiency, artistry, and inherited knowledge of the independent landowner or tradesman. Work in the factories and corporations of this early twentieth-century world was both more lucrative and more tedious than that of previous generations. This phenomenon—the experience of work—ushered in an era of leisure and mobility as young people focused on spending their newfound time and money in satisfying weekend pursuits. Gone were the days of the Victorian values of thrift, modesty, and social hierarchies. The emerging era was characterized by the exhilarating entertainments of popular culture, such as movies, automobile racing, and boxing. This man saw the potential in all this. As part of this cultural transformation, he dreamed of a "horseless carriage" that would be affordable to all of these leisure-seekers, even the most lowly factory worker. His name, of course, was Henry Ford.

Today, it is easy to forget how unique Ford's vision for a "universal horseless carriage" was back at the turn of the last century. At the time that he was tinkering with his various models, Detroit was filled with hundreds of other engineers and mechanics just like him, all chasing the same dream of developing the winning prototype for an automobile. In fact, Ford was by no means the most talented engineer, nor was he the most capable manager. Several of his early "horseless carriage" start-ups went belly up because he couldn't deliver on time to his investors. What characterized Ford's unique vision—his creative breakthrough—was his awareness of the needs and desires of this emerging leisure class. Several of his wealthiest investors pressured him to create car models that were aimed at the luxury markets. Such vehicles would serve as mere novelties, showpieces for the elite. Ford, a committed populist, refused the needling of his shareholders. He only grew more determined to make a car that would open up mobility—and consumption—for all. Ford saw that in this new America, moving up and out would be a fundamental part of life—and the car would be instrumental in this.

To achieve his vision, he needed to find a less expensive system for assembling cars. Ford, like Eliot, saw what others around him did not. In passing by a slaughterhouse and watching workers on an assembly line cut up pigs into their component parts—he had a flash of insight. This same type of assembly line could work for building cars; it would be cheaper and much faster than making them piecemeal.

When Ford introduced the Model T in 1908, there were only about 18,000 miles of paved road in the U.S. His cars were lightweight, easy to repair and maintain and, most importantly, affordable at around $825 each. His company sold 15 million Model Ts before they stopped production in 1927. It was the catalyst for an entirely new lifestyle in America, revolving around the twin values of mobility and consumption.

Although it might seem strange to begin this chapter by drawing a parallel between Eliot and Ford—between one of the greatest poets in the English language and America's most famous industrialist—they share a similar gift of sensitivity. Both men were able to attune to the *mood* of modernity. One pessimistic and the other fiercely optimistic, Eliot and Ford revealed entirely new and theretofore unimaginable possibilities for their worlds. Their shared genius was in staying open to insights, and it is exemplary of the creativity that is at the heart of the sensemaking process. Let's take some time to look more carefully at how this occurs. With phenomenology as our guide, we can ask: How do humans *actually* experience creativity?

Grace & Will

Grace

How do we talk about creativity in everyday language? We say: I *got* an idea. It *came* to me. It *dawned* on me. We don't say: I *made* an idea or I *took* an idea. This seemingly minor semantic observation is actually quite telling. We experience ideas as phenomena coming to us from the outside rather than something we generate from within.

Ideas are like gifts that the world bestows on us rather than creations we summon through force of will when we need them. Of course, there is labor involved in idea generation. People have to train and focus on their chosen craft—if you haven't done decades of mathematical proofs, it is unlikely that you will receive an insight into solving a world-famous theorem. After the work is done, however, and the proverbial ten thousand hours of practice have been clocked, we have no active control over our insights.

This is why I choose the word *grace* when I describe the phenomenon of the creative process. Although the word *grace* tends to evoke the presence of the divine, my definition has nothing to do with religion or spirituality. For me, *grace* is a word that characterizes us when we are both active and receptive to our worlds. It acknowledges that insights are about remaining open to our environment, open to understanding other people and other cultures. Creative insights do not come "from us." Rather, they travel "through us" from the social sphere in which we live. Great artists, writers, musicians, inventors, and entrepreneurs know this already. Famed psychologist

Wolfgang Köhler once described the "three Bs" of creativity: the bus, the bath, and the bed. All three are places where creativity reveals itself, because they are environments where we are typically in a receptive state of being.

Heidegger calls this act of revealing or bringing to light *phainesthai*. Though this ancient Greek verb may strike modern readers as obscure, for Heidegger it was the only word that actually captured the phenomenon of creativity. You see, in ancient Greek, *phainesthai* uses the "middle voice"; this is a voice in the Greek language that is neither entirely active nor entirely passive. It characterizes us when we are at one with our environment, indistinguishable from the equipment and the chains of meaning that make up our existence. Like grace, *phainesthai* erases the distinction between subject and object; it is neither what things do on their own nor what we do to them, but rather what happens in our engagement *with* them. In this way, things are revealed *through* us, not *by* us.

Some of you are probably thinking: enough with the semantics. But stay with me. How we conceive of creativity and the words we use to describe it actually do have real-world implications for our everyday lives. When we use the wrong model for the phenomenon of creativity, we begin to value the wrong things. We fail to anticipate nonlinear change; we dull our natural abilities to extract meaning from qualitative information; and we compartmentalize our learning and knowledge into atomized silos. In short, we lose sight of the holistic thinking that characterizes sensemaking.

Still not satisfied? As you read on in this chapter, I will introduce you to some of the most creative minds I know and show you their creative processes—using phenomenology to describe them—to give you a more nuanced description of this final phase of sensemaking.

Before I begin, however, I need to take you on a slight detour to show you how we continue to get creativity wrong.

Will

If *grace* is an accurate word for how we actually experience creativity, *will* is the word that is too often associated with creative breakthroughs. Many of us consider ideas the guaranteed outcome of a mental assembly line: by following a rigid process, we can manufacture creativity every single time. When we *will* ideas into being, we crank them out. We treat ideas as discrete and atomized widgets that we can then fabricate into an existence apart from any context. *Will* harkens back to our critique of Descartes. It implies that we sit detached from our worlds—subjects apart from objects—in analytical thought.

One of the most egregious examples of this misconception of creativity comes from our current fixation with design thinking. If a Silicon Valley state of mind is dominated by its obsessions with the hard sciences, this alternative Bay Area culture is characterized by its religious devotion to the "design process." Though this culture conceives of itself as the creative and artsy alternative to the engineers that dominate Silicon Valley, its ideology of willful creativity is no less corrosive to our intellectual values. What is "design thinking" exactly? Despite what its proponents would have us believe, it has nothing to do with humanities thinking. Allow me to give you an anatomy of design thinking, or what I like to call "the bullshit tornado."

Design Thinking: The Anatomy of a Bullshit Tornado

Over the past twenty years, designers have taken a remarkable leap in status. They used to be craftsmen interested in shapes, materials, and fonts. Today, they are oracles with solutions for everything from social security to crime prevention to the eradication of malaria. What knowledge endows them with the authority to opine on all of these subjects? According to design thinking, no knowledge at all. The ideology claims that it is their lack of expertise that allows them to connect with consumers. Designers believe that they alone are best suited to create user-friendly products because they are unencumbered by an intellectual background in any specific context—economics or political science or anthropology. Even highly complex and historically created ideas like the welfare state are a "design" in this ideology. World hunger? Education reform? Yes, you guessed it: "design problems." And the solution to them is always the same: design thinking.

The most famous design firm—a mecca for design thinking— is IDEO, founded by David Kelley, the current head of Stanford's Institute of Design, or d-school. IDEO is the oft-cited design firm behind ubiquitous household items such as the Apple mouse, PalmPilot's Palm V, and stand-up toothpaste tubes. The firm was featured in a profile on *Nightline* in 1999, and the eight-minute segment manages to touch on almost every aspect of design thinking that makes it unhelpful to authentic creative endeavors.

1. Innovation without Any Social Context

"We're not actually experts at any given area," David Kelley tells *Nightline*. "We are experts on the process of how you design stuff. So we don't care if you give us a toothbrush, a toothpaste tube, a tractor, a space shuttle, a chair. . . . it's all the same to us. We want to figure out how to innovate by using our process and applying it."

Let's step back and consider these words for just one moment: *a toothbrush, a toothpaste tube, a tractor, a space shuttle, a chair. . . . it's all the same to us.* Is it, though? Should it be? Do you really want the designers of NASA's next space shuttle to use the same roadmap as the designers of a tube of toothpaste? In IDEO's design-thinking model, ideas are conceived of as modular pieces, completely separate from the person having the idea and the social world in which that idea was created. These types of ideas—atomized and modular—are not painful to change or explain because they carry such a low bandwidth of information. Having an idea is free, and killing an idea carries no risk.

But humans exist in worlds, and the objects within those worlds are always context-dependent and layered with meaning, so David Kelley's statement is misguided at best. It is impossible to extract a space shuttle from the context of travel into outer space and the bounty of knowledge necessary to design it. Space travel—including astronauts and rocket scientists along with all the other engineers and objects that make up their world—has a completely different culture from that of farmers and tractors, or the culture of an American family standing around their bathroom sink at bedtime. Unless we know what truly matters to astronauts, farmers, or children attempting to brush their teeth, we cannot really understand anything at all about the objects—or equipment—that they use. And we certainly cannot presume to know what might make that equipment serve them better.

2. *Ignorance Is Bliss*

Another salient aspect of design thinking is highlighted on a *60 Minutes* segment from 2013 featuring IDEO: expertise and experience hinder innovation. IDEO likes to "throw doctors, opera singers, and engineers into a room and get them to brainstorm." In design thinking, anyone can have an idea and ideas can come from anywhere. They favor diversity in the group brainstorming sessions because they feel that different perspectives will come up with more of their signature "wild ideas." But in what world will these wild ideas be relevant? They might appear innovative to the world of designers, but how will they have any resonance without knowledge of the actual social contexts in which these products and services will be used? Process is clearly more important than product.

Process is so sacred at IDEO, in fact, that they like to repeat the mantra "Defer judgment." According to the *Nightline* feature, someone dings a bell when another member of the group is criticizing a brainstorm idea early on. In this way, expertise is seen as a potential creativity blocker. The priority is a process where "ideas pour out and are posted on the walls." Less important, it seems, is what is actually written on all those Post-it notes.

3. Get Under the Skin of Consumers

Being "customer-centric" is paramount for design thinkers like IDEO. Not that they have any real interest in leaving their studios in hip cities to go out and explore other worlds. But they love to talk about empathy and how it is necessary for the design of exciting products. They will tell you that by getting "under the skin" of the consumer, "you can learn how they 'tick and click' and then get them to love [not just like or buy] your brand, your idea, and your soul." Then they will go back upstairs to their studios and get back to their passionate work.

The proponents of design thinking defend the ideology by saying that they spend time with people, observing and empathizing with their circumstances. But I liken this to "drive-by" anthropology. The time they spend is quite limited—often only an afternoon—and they approach their period of observation with a predetermined goal: How can I "improve" the design of this one individual object? With this narrow goal in mind, design thinkers never fully immerse themselves in the world of the subjects. It is no surprise, then, that everything coming out of design firms looks alike today. It's a San Francisco designers' world—soft shapes in varying shades of white—and the rest of us are just living in it. Only when we give ourselves over to our shared social context will different worlds and their practices reveal themselves.

4. Remove All Pain

Design thinking at firms like IDEO claims to map out all the "pain points" a consumer might have using a product or a service. If you want to make a better yogurt, for example, designers look at all the problems someone might have in finding, choosing, opening, and eating a yogurt. Though this might at first strike you as a relatively pain*less* process, designers would disagree. There are pains around finding the yogurt in the supermarket, pains around a lack of emotional connection with the yogurt, and pains around opening the yogurt package without getting yogurt all over your hands. Once all the pains have been mapped out, design thinking follows a process to redesign the experience to make it entirely anesthetizing. Designers might suggest, for example, adding a sensor to the yogurt so that you can find it immediately with your yogurt app, or a personalization of the yogurt so that it carries your name and your uploaded profile picture on it. Design thinking might discover a new way to design the packaging of the yogurt so that any mess is efficiently whisked away by a cutting-edge polymer scrim.

Through this exact same process, design thinking promises to eliminate pain points in all of the social structures in our worlds: government, the economy, mass transit. Perhaps there is a polymer scrim to eliminate pain points in our electoral system? Design thinking's ultimate goal is to identify all of life's pains and remove them through a nirvana of better design.

5. The Wall of Warm Words

As design thinking conceives of itself as the warm and fuzzy alternative to the hard-nosed scientific culture in Silicon Valley, proponents like to throw around humanities-inspired words to describe their "vibe." You will likely hear some combination of the following words and phrases in any design-thinking conversation: holistic, creative, team-oriented, people-centric, visionary, disruptive, agile, fast. You will hear that we can change the world—but, unlike the engineering conversation down the hall, this change will "put humans back at the center." You will hear that the future belongs to crowds and that we must let go of the notion of the lonely genius. There will almost certainly be some reference to a salmon swimming upstream, and "passion" will be evoked throughout the conversation.

In the world of wine, there are rules for what you can say about yourself and your products. Only wine made from grapes grown in Burgundy can be called Burgundy wine. In farming, only organically grown English peas can be labeled organic. In the world of design thinking, however, regulations and restraining rules are nonexistent. The wall of warm words serves, instead, to connote authority. As expertise carries little value, anyone and everyone can claim to be a "strategist," an "experience designer," or a "keynote speaker." These various phrases and titles all have the same underlying meaning in design thinking: *If you don't want to be Ubered, you need to listen to designers.*

6. The Return to the B-school Parking Lot

Lest this wall of warm words become *too* warm, design thinking also requires casual references from the world of business: "leverage," "ROI," or "business model." The idea is that the creative process might be a wild and crazy joyride, but the stolen car will always return to the business school parking lot. Throwing around concepts like "the four Ps" and "five forces" reassures everyone that pragmatism and reason are really at the heart of the work.

—— ⁕ ——

Of course it's not just IDEO. The tyranny of "willed" creativity that comes from design thinking is all around us and it now forms a prevalent part of the business culture's conversation around innovation. Robert Sutton, the author of *Weird Ideas That Work,* tells his readers: "In the creative process, ignorance is bliss."

One might even go so far as to argue that this particular model of creativity takes its inspiration from Rousseau's philosophy: we are at our most creative when we are naïve and innocent, unfettered by pesky rules and authoritarian expertise. "It's now time to party," writes the author of the book *How to Have Kick-Ass Ideas,* Chris Baréz-Brown, as he draws a direct connection between playfulness and creative genius. "So the message is, when in doubt, say '*Na na na-na na*' and laugh at the world."

Baréz-Brown's book—representative of much of the literature today on creative thinking—is written like a storybook for preschool children. The enemy of playfulness, in the author's view, is the collection of experts and people who claim to "know a lot." He calls them "*clever clever thinky thinky*" people.

Such language connotes playfulness with liberation. It implies that work is enslaving our thoughts: the office is a place where we are treated like faceless bureaucrats while our expertise and knowledge is blinding us. To be creative, we need to free ourselves from the bonds of corporate bureaucracy, expertise, and rational analysis. True liberation exists in the world of a child: open, playful, curious, and spontaneous.

Recently, I had the opportunity to spend the day with one of these "childlike" creatives: "Martin." I wish I could say that I had never met a "Martin" before but, unfortunately, in my world they show up in almost any conversation that involves creative thinking. Martins are people who eschew the painstakingly hard work of observing reality for easy buzzwords and empty status plays. Martins prey on fear: when everyone in the room is anxious about their careers, about their industries, and about the general state of "disruptive innovation," Martins waltz in and play shaman.

More than anything, Martins remind me that creative thinking and brilliant innovation require engaging with a process that is extremely hard and, honestly, quite unsettling. There is no money-back guarantee, no predetermined roadmap; in fact, getting lost is the whole point. The Martins of my world represent procrastination because the actual work—the truth of making sense of the world—requires good old-fashioned thinking. This is something the Martins stopped doing long ago.

Martin Solves the Problems

I was working with a strategy team for a global clothing company and we were all on the last leg of a whirlwind trip from Paris to London and, now, New York. Over the course of five days, all of us—twenty different executives and our consulting group—had been exposed to the cultures in each of the different cities. We had just one day left to finish outlining the contours of their new strategy and to complete the future product profile for the upcoming year.

Then entered Martin.

Martin was a new but senior recruit to the company's local design outpost in New York. He showed up in perfectly distressed dark jeans with tattoos up his arms; he was probably in his early thirties and exuded a calm charisma. The rest of us had all started at 9 AM on that final day, but Martin floated in at two in the afternoon.

The company's leader, Axel, a man responsible for all of the company's global strategy, interrupted our discussion to welcome Martin. Axel was genuinely worried about his job. His company was number two in the category, but losing market share every month. They were especially out of touch with the youth in big cities of Western Europe and the United States, and Axel needed to understand why. One of his bets was to bring in Martin, a star designer recruited from their competitor.

"We are so happy to have local representatives help us shape our new strategy," Axel told all of us in the group.

"Well, I'm certainly also honored to be here today," Martin responded. Now that he had the informal permission to speak, he felt compelled to go on. "What I sense in this room is intensity and passion. Passion for the brand you are part of. Passion is important; passion is what drives our brand forward. You as a group have that passion, but also as individuals. Appreciate what you have here. It's energy. And it's an important energy. An energy that drives the brand forward. Without having the time and commitment to have these intense, passionate discussions about the brand, we cannot develop it. It cannot evolve. You are here as a team, with dedicated time to shape the future of our brand. And you each contribute with passion and energy. I hope you appreciate this. I feel you appreciate this. Because it's important."

The atmosphere in the room was welcoming, open. Martin continued: "I am here to contribute. But in order for me to do so I need to know who you are, where you're from, what's your story. Could we do a quick round of introductions?"

Everybody in the room introduced themselves; the entire process took probably twenty minutes. The facilitator nervously looked at his watch. The schedule for this session was already a bit delayed, but the new member of the team did not seem concerned with time. Every time a member of the team introduced him- or herself, Martin followed up with a question.

"Now," Martin said after the round of introductions. "I get you now. I get you as individuals, I get you as a group, and I understand why each of you is passionate about our brand. But I don't get your journey. You've seen places. Paris, London, New York. You've met people shaping your view on things during this journey. Help me onboard this journey. If I'm supposed to contribute constructively, I need to understand your context. I need to understand the unmet needs of people, their pain points. Could you please take me through your experiences so far? Who did you meet, what did you discuss with them, what did you take away from your encounters?"

The facilitator suggested that someone fill Martin in on all of this in the next break. Axel, the leader, agreed: "It is great to have you on board. We appreciate you taking the time to be with us and your willingness to contribute. I think we need to continue with what we were doing before you came. Please help us the best you can and someone from the team will give you a more in-depth update in a break."

Martin ignored the plea to get the program of the day back on track from the leader. "Don't forget the intensity it takes to bring the brand forward. Don't forget how much it means that you are here, assembled as a team, working together as a team. We can change the lives of the consumers. We can design for their pain points and surprise and delight them. If we don't, we will be left behind."

Most of the team in the room looked at Martin with smiles. He instinctively took the role of the charismatic priest. With his face tilted upward in calm reflection, he communicated to all of us that he accepted his role as coach for the collective.

A few people, however, including Axel, were growing uncomfortable. They wanted to remain polite, but they were getting restless to shift the focus away from Martin and back to strategic thinking.

"Our brand is more than ninety years old," Martin said. "And what our old colleagues have built, they have built with passion and dedication. We are standing on their shoulders and our mission is to bring the brand forward. That is why we are all here. We touch millions of people every day with our brand, we have the power to touch and change the lives of millions. But the times have changed. We live in the age of crowds and sharing economy. The revolution of the economy—the fourth revolution—is bigger than what anyone has ever seen. We will have digital highways and more money will be made in the coming years than in the past decades."

Martin took a pause for dramatic effect. He seemed to summon the next phrases from a deeply soulful place inside himself. "The millennial generation and data lakes will change everything we know. Just look at Apple or Uber. We don't want to be like the taxi drivers that have been disrupted, do we guys?"

It all sounded somehow both tantalizing and scary, but what did it mean in practice? Axel couldn't help taking a few notes despite his fears about the time. He wrote down "data lakes" and "disrupted taxi drivers" with thick underlines in his notebook.

"Let's continue building on that foundation and take it into a new era," Martin seemed poised to go on indefinitely.

"Time for group work, guys," the facilitator interrupted him. "Think about what Martin shared with us in your next exercise, and Martin, you will join team two."

And with that, Martin let go of his grip of the group and joined the program. But his willingness to obey the rules was short-lived. Every time the teams assembled again as a whole after teamwork, Martin was never shy about speaking up.

At 6:30 PM, everyone was tired. It was the fifth day in a row with workshops and heated debates, and time to wrap up and go for dinner. The facilitator thanked everybody for the hard work and the achievements so far.

"I also want to thank you," Martin told the room while people were packing their bags. Everyone was desperate to get out of the cluttered workshop room with the stale air, but the urgency didn't stop Martin from speaking. "I want to thank you for letting me join these important discussions. Discussions about our future. Discussions about where we are going. Passionate discussions where the team gets together and talks. The passion I sense in this room, on this day, should not just wither away and die. It should be kept alive. Because it is discussions like these that keep the brand alive."

————⌥————

Most of us have probably met at least one or two Martins in our careers: so-called big shots with shortsighted assumptions, superficial mastery of jargon, and an inexhaustible hubris for hijacking creative discourse. For those of us in the business of trying to discover the truth about the world, Martin's nonsense is an infuriating waste of time.

But if creativity has nothing to do with gurus like Martin or the guaranteed delivery of the design-thinking factory, how do we develop a relationship to a sustained creative process? What is sensemaking if we have no control over the results? After all, I am running a company filled with people. At a certain point, I need to achieve meaningful insights for myself and for my clients. We try to live in a receptive state of being, but we also need to develop a way to articulate our process to ourselves as well as to our clients.

I asked my colleagues and partners to share how they arrived at their most creative thinking. The following descriptions are strikingly different in procedure but they all contain an element of immersion: an empathic dive into another world. Instead of forgoing context, they embrace it. This thick data—stories, anecdotes, and analysis—characterizes the phenomenon I call *grace*.

1. Charlie

I need to be deeply immersed in the phenomenon I am dealing with for each and every project. For example, right now I need to understand tea in China. What does tea mean to the Chinese?

What are their everyday relationships to tea? How are they treating it, talking about it, paying for it, giving it to each other? This immersion is not one directed effort; it is more like walking in the landscape of tea rather than memorizing everything about tea.

After I have read, talked, observed, and listened for long enough (it never is, but when I am hearing things for the third time, I am okay with stopping the discovery process), I always do the following: I leave my notes, my computer, and the data behind. I wait a day while I allow my thoughts to drift elsewhere. I go to the movies or meet friends. This seems strange at the most intense point of the project, but without a short break, I always fail. Then, after a day and a night of good sleep without once letting myself think about tea, I just take one piece of paper and a pen. I like Bic pens and white sheets of paper. I go to a place that's loud and crowded. Coffee shops work. So do bars or very busy restaurants. I sit down in the public place and I write down whatever comes to mind.

The strange thing about this process is that the enforced break filters the thousands of ideas I have been studying. I don't think about order or importance. I just write down what my pen seems to want to write. What comes out always ends up being the strongest ideas and the most organized thoughts. It seems like the body or the subconscious or whatever organizes everything for me and cuts through all the clutter. On that one piece of paper is a condensed version, the essence of an idea. I can then take that idea and move it in any direction I need to explain it in great fidelity. But the core of it always comes out. It seems haphazard to have multimillion-dollar projects work like this, but that is actually how I work.

It has nothing to do with me, by the way. It doesn't feel like I'm the one writing things down. I am not some kind of lone genius. I just respect my body and know that it will do this if I am open and let it. I wouldn't know any other way to arrive at creative ideas.

2. Mikkel

I have a painful relationship with the process of generating ideas. I always panic. I feel like I am sure to fail every time a deadline is getting close. Which it always is. It feels like I have knives in my stomach, like I am going to show the world that I really am a failure and not creative at all. My sleep gets disturbed. I feel nauseous. Even when I am working on things that aren't as important to me, I am afraid that it will finally be obvious to everyone that I am worthless.

Eventually, the knives get worse and worse. Then I start producing, circling around the idea over and over again. I am wearing myself down, trying this and then trying that. I overproduce. I panic and try and try again. I go at the problem with such force that I hope I can break it. It is very unpleasant for everyone around me. They can see it is existential for me. I have lost a lot of great employees this way. I am still waiting for the time when it doesn't work and the world will see that I am a loser.

Somehow, while I have been distracted by all of this misery, an idea appears. It usually comes right at the moment when I feel like I am going to vomit up these knives. This idea didn't come from me. It simply arrived when I was too weak and distracted to shut it out.

I then describe the idea over and over again to others. It's nuts. I talk and talk at people, not with them. I could talk to a wall, but people are better for me. Those poor people. From there, I use people with other skills to describe the idea. After all this pain and torture, my sleep returns and my stomach is okay again.

3. Charlotte

I get all my ideas when I am running. Not during, but right after. Running somehow empties my head. I have tried cycling and long walks and they're okay, but not as good. I need running to completely empty my mind of thoughts. When I have been working on a problem for a long time, I am immersed in the topic up to my chin. Somehow the emptying of the mind makes everything fall into place. It feels like something sends me the idea in a clear format. It doesn't feel like it's me. It is more like someone else is organizing my thoughts. It's so strange, and it doesn't always work. I guess some people say they sleep on ideas or decisions; I run on them.

4. Jun

I am tormented by my clients. I am so afraid of losing them or letting them down. They are the ones with the real risk, and I am just their best bet at some kind of help.

I have never thought about my process in this way before, but in reality I am trying to think like my clients. How would they react? When I do this for a while, and especially when I am close to a deadline, I somehow turn into them. It isn't just that I try to think about what they would think or do. I am them. I react emotionally to ideas and thoughts like they would; I feel the world like they feel it. It's like being a ghost or something. My body, my soul, is no longer mine; it has been occupied by the people I am trying to help. It's not about help anymore—more of a complete immersion. I see their ghosts, I feel their fear of failure. It's a little like what shamans do. Perhaps it's that experience.

Getting ideas doesn't make me happy. It's work. It's deep, intense, and hard work.

For all their differences in process, what these descriptions of graceful creativity share is the same experience of receptivity, the openness, the being at one with the world. I hear and see these same characterizations every time I speak or read about a genuinely creative process. This state of grace is a universal experience for sensemaking insights.

Consider just a few other examples from across business, literature, and the arts:

I don't know where great ideas come from. I am not sure anyone does. I am not even sure how I come up with my ideas. The brain does its thing, and out pops an idea.

While you are waiting for the brain to get its act together, do what you can do. Do the doable. Meet with people, schmooze, have a laugh or two. Build mockups and prototypes. At the very least, collect other people's problems. That's always a guaranteed doable.

The deep idea here is that action has a creative aspect distinct from thinking. And thinking need not come first. Mostly it doesn't.

—*Saras D. Sarasvathy,* professor of Business Administration at University of Virginia's Darden School of Business

Why is it I always get my best ideas while shaving?

—*Albert Einstein*

Plots come to me at such odd moments: when I am walking along a street, or examining a hat-shop with particular interest, suddenly a splendid idea comes into my head, and I think, "Now that would be a neat way of covering up the crime so that nobody would see the point." Of course, all the practical details are still to be worked out, and the people have to creep slowly into my consciousness, but I jot down my splendid idea in an exercise book.

—Agatha Christie

I drive people crazy, but I need to feel it. Leadership is what happens when management models and linear thinking ends. I need to feel what is right. Sometimes that takes time, but I am okay with that. I can move very fast when I feel something is right.

Often when I have done my thinking, I just know something needs to be done. We have invested in computer science and data analytics without having a clear business goal. It turns out that that might be the best investment we have made in a long time. But when we did it, it was because it felt important and necessary. Not because we had a business case. It is obvious now, but wasn't when we did it.

Clarity comes when I wake up. What I have been pondering for a while is suddenly clear. It really is not very well understood how this happens, but I wake up, and can clearly see what was murky yesterday. You basically just know.

—Mark Fields, CEO of Ford

The participant enters into the mind of the market and tries to understand it from the inside...I assumed the market felt the same way as I did, and by keeping myself detached from other personal feelings I could sense changes in its mood. This was a hard discipline. It meant subordinating my own emotions to those of the market.

—*George Soros*

I would say to her, "This time don't go full throttle," and before you knew it, she was on the floor with tears coming down her cheeks—it was like she has some open conduit where the themes and ideas of the play come through her, and you just can't stop it.

—*Theater director Tina Landau's description of working with actress Phylicia Rashad*

So much in writing depends on the superficiality of one's days. One may be preoccupied with shopping and income tax returns and chance conversations, but the stream of the unconscious continues to flow undisturbed, solving problems, planning ahead: one sits down sterile and dispirited at the desk, and suddenly the words come as though from the air: the situations that seemed blocked in a hopeless impasse move forward: the work has been done while one slept or shopped or talked with friends.

—*Graham Greene*, The End of the Affair

When the mind is occupied with a monotonous task, it can stimulate the subconscious into a eureka moment.

That's what happened to me. The business model for my company, Clearfit, which provides an easy way for companies to find employees and predict job fit, hatched in the back of my mind while I was driving 80 miles an hour, not thinking about work at all.

The subconscious mind runs in the background, silently affecting the outcome of many thoughts. So, take a break and smell the flowers, because while you're out doing that, your mind may very well solve the problem that you are trying to solve or spark a solution to a problem you hadn't considered before.

—Ben Baldwin, co-founder and CEO, Clearfit

Don't be afraid to be confused. Try to remain permanently confused. Anything is possible. Stay open, forever, so open it hurts, and then open up some more, until the day you die, world without end, amen.

—George Saunders, "The Braindead Megaphone"

What do creative geniuses like writer George Saunders mean when they say "open"? This receptive state requires remaining unattached to preconceptions, expectations, and biases. This is no small order. Ancient Buddhists in Japan found that young monks had such difficulty staying open that they created a whole philosophical discipline around it. Buddhist priest Zenkei Blanche Hartman referred to this concept of the "beginner's mind" in one of her lectures from 2001:

It is the mind that is innocent of preconceptions and expectations, judgments and prejudices. I think of beginner's mind as the mind that faces life like a small child, full of curiosity and wonder and amazement. "I wonder what this is? I wonder what that is? I wonder what this means?" Without approaching things with a fixed point of view or a prior judgment, just asking, "What is it?"

Whether it is the experience of running, the ritual of putting pen to paper, or the tortured exercise of imagining knives, creative thinkers all develop techniques to keep themselves open to ideas. Needless to say, it is incredibly difficult for us as humans to stay receptive. Our minds long to weave patterns, to create order from chaos, and to return to some sense of certainty. But the longer we can sit productively in this place of "not knowing," the more we make ourselves available to insight.

The concept of abductive reasoning can further illuminate how this works. Charles Sanders Peirce, the nineteenth-century American philosopher and logician, famously defined abduction in relationship to two other types of reasoning we use to problem solve: deduction and induction.

Deduction is essentially the domain of algorithms. You start with a hypothetical set of beliefs and, from there, deduce that X or Y is true. It is often called the "top-down" approach because it goes from the more general to the more specific.

Induction, on the other hand, begins with a collection of multiple premises that then lead to a specific conclusion. This is why it is referred to as "bottom-up": it goes from specific observations to broader generalizations and theories.

Abduction: Abductive reasoning, however, does not start with any hypothesis or even preconceived notions about what is known or unknown. In this way, it is the only method of reasoning that can incorporate new knowledge and insights. The process begins by casting a wide net for data collection and organization—the "openness" that George Saunders describes. Then the patterns from the data collection are identified. Once these patterns are synthesized, a theory or several theories begin to take shape. From these theories, an insight emerges with explanatory power. Here's Peirce from his 1903 Harvard lecture on "Pragmatism and Abduction":

> The abductive suggestion comes to us like a flash but it is not a flash available to all. It is an act of insight, although of extremely fallible insight. It is true that the different elements of the hypothesis were in our minds before; but it is the idea of putting together what we had never before dreamed of putting together, which flashes the new suggestion before our contemplation.

Peirce argued that abductive reasoning is the only appropriate process for messy and evasive data. It is where true creativity lies. Unfortunately, it is also where great fallibility lies. This is why masters who experience "grace" learn how to recognize the sensation of a worthwhile creative insight. The nineteenth-century philosopher William James argued in his seminal book, *The Principles of Psychology*, that this practice is largely cultivated through the force of our sustained attention:

Attention...is the taking possession by the mind, in clear and vivid form, of one out of what seem several simultaneously possible objects or trains of thought. Focalization, concentration, of consciousness are of its essence. It implies withdrawal from some things in order to deal effectively with others, and is a condition which has a real opposite in the confused, dazed, scatterbrained state which in French is called *distraction,* and *Zerstreutheit* in German.

In other words, creative thinkers understand that what they are attuned to—what is revealed to them in a state of grace—is what allows them to achieve an understanding in the world. "Millions of items of the outward order are present to my senses which never properly enter into my experience," James writes. "Why? Because they have no interest for me. My experience is what I agree to attend to."

At the height of her brain injury, Nicole Pollentier described walking through Target, overwhelmed by the chaotic indiscriminateness of her experience. She was incapable of attending to anything, a process she described as "filtering."

"My working memory was damaged so it was like a waiting room that was overflowing," she recalled. "Normally, when your brain is working at its normal speed, filtering happens instantaneously. We don't know most of what we're filtering all the time."

By contrast, according to James, the experience of a genius on the cusp of a breakthrough is that of a sustained attention: "Their ideas coruscate, every subject branches infinitely before their fertile minds, and so for hours they may be rapt." James describes how these minds are "furnished" with materials.

These are the nooks and crannies into which their infinite branches might grow. And the more the minds are furnished— the more we have read, experienced, and contemplated—the more material we have to work with when an opportunity arises for a creative breakthrough. Though these breakthroughs might happen "in a flash," the reality is that they are based on a rich depth of knowledge in pattern recognition.

In his famous book from 2011, *Thinking, Fast and Slow*, psychologist Daniel Kahneman wrote that the more knowledge we have stored away—the furnishings of our minds—the more adept we are at these so-called fast flashes of intuition, what he dubbed System 1 thinking. As William James put it, geniuses "differ from ordinary men less in the character of their attention than in the nature of the objects upon which it is successively bestowed."

The most creative people in the world, then, are the most open to what is being revealed or shown to them by their world. This is an essential element of grace: the moment when we suddenly understand exactly where to put our attention. Masters are particularly skilled at recognizing it. Take the world-famous architect Bjarke Ingels: he felt a call of creative insight when he witnessed the inner workings of a meticulously crafted Swiss watch.

Flash of Insight: The Click

It was winter 2013, and Bjarke Ingels was driving through the western part of Switzerland, past the ski resorts and then down into the Vallée de Joux of the Jura mountain range. There, amid snow and mountains beside the beautiful Lac de Joux, he arrived at the legendary Swiss watchmaking company Audemars Piguet, the only Swiss watchmaking company still owned by the same family after 150 years. Ingels and his team were preparing a bid to create a structure that would extend the company's historic buildings as well as add on a new museum to showcase their collection of hundreds of fine watches. Any viable bid would need to honor their traditions as a company of storied artisans as well as create a dynamic conversation with the two historic buildings—each one close to one hundred years old—already in place at the site.

Only in his early forties, Bjarke Ingels initially struck many members of the Audemars Piguet family as the wildcard in the architectural competition. Ingels is not lacking in prestige or experience: between his original offices in Copenhagen and his newer offices in New York City and London, the Bjarke Ingels Group, or BIG, is in the midst of completing dozens of new buildings all over the world, in cities as diverse as Vancouver; Faroe Islands; Hualien (Taiwan); Shenzhen, China; and New York City. The firm has won a bevy of international prizes and awards. What makes BIG stand out is their approach to the creative process, which is fundamentally different from that of other world-famous studios. Ingels's work, replete with undulating loops and slopes, often defies all the traditional architectural dimensions and conventions—all the *ideas* of what a building should be.

Though his team had already put together several possible strategies, Ingels traveled to the headquarters in Switzerland because he needed to experience the context of the site in person. He was looking for something in the visit that would give him the "click," the sense of everything coming together into a design that would capture what makes a 150-year-old Swiss watchmaking company so special.

"With a click, the left and the right get equally satisfied," Ingels told me when I asked him about his creative process. "There are so many crossovers that it crystallizes into something that makes sense. In fact, it makes so much sense that it couldn't be any different. You just couldn't answer it any other way."

Considering Switzerland's relationship to craftsmanship, Ingels knew he could build something of quality. He also had tremendous respect for the precision involved in watchmaking. Despite these more cerebral threads, however, he did not yet have a visceral connection to the project.

In the course of his studio tour, Ingels began chatting with a Catalan watchmaker, a man in his late fifties who worked for Audemars Piguet. The artisan was working on historic timepieces and walking Ingels through the mechanics of his process. As Ingels put it, "After talking with that watchmaker—looking at his hands and his tools and really seeing how precise and meticulous his work was—suddenly, the penny dropped and I got really excited. I could really feel it." Ingels's moment of revelation—what Heidegger calls *phainesthai*—was his feeling for the craft itself: extracting so much performance out of so little material. "First you have to fall in love with the subject you are designing for, and once you have that, you can channel the feeling into all the things you need to deliver. But deliver in a way that manifests aspects of the culture of watchmaking."

Ingels was particularly intrigued by the engineering involved in the mainspring of the watch. "The anchor swings around and stores the kinetic energy of your body in this mainspring: a piece of metal that is wound up by the anchor swinging around. This is a force that it then delivers back to the clock. And there is a regulator that makes sure it's not just unfolding in one go but is unwinding in these bursts that you can use to then show you time. I suddenly understood that in watchmaking, as in architecture, the design, or the form, *is* the content. It's the way that the material is organized that makes the clock show the time."

He used this conceit of the mainspring as the metaphor for the entire museum. Watchmakers have to select their materials to maximum effect using a minimum of matter, and he wanted this museum—called the Maison des Fondateurs (home of the founders)—to do the same. The new building needed to take visitors down a long path that showed them the history and the culture of watchmaking. Ingels and his team had initially conceived of this path in the museum as something long and linear. The moment he saw the mainspring in the hands of the Catalan watchmaker, however, he realized he could use a completely different shape for the construction: a double spiral. "The spiral takes you into the beginning of the museum and then takes you out, almost like the coil that stores the energy of the watch."

Once the strategy was set, it was clear they needed a lightweight steel structure to create the shape of the overlapping spirals. The choice of a lighter material allows the building to rise, seemingly weightless, out of the surrounding landscape of the Vallée de Joux. Taking inspiration from the engineering of the mainspring, the model has no walls or load-bearing structures other than windows. These windows, made of technically advanced glass, hold up the roof.

When Ingels presented the design, there was immediate excitement from Audemars Piguet. BIG is known
for audaciousness, but here, as in other projects, the der-
ring-do is actually in service of site constraints. The complications BIG's building brings to the project—only
high-performing glass to hold up the entire structure,
for example—resonate with the "grand complications"
like moon phases and annual calendars embedded in the
mechanics of fine art watches. BIG officially won the
competition among five firms invited to submit designs and
construction is set to begin in the next few years.

Most world-famous architects have a signature style at the
core of their practice. Take modernist master Ludwig Mies
van der Rohe as an example: his buildings are easy to recognize by their elegant structure and rich, dark brown colors.
Mies, like Frank Gehry and Rem Koolhaas, essentially relied
on one formula for most of his buildings regardless of the use,
context, and economics. These architects arrived at each and
every site with a desire to build the beautiful structure they
envisioned.

Ingels's process—illustrative of a sensemaking that all
masters engage in—is different. BIG doesn't rely on a codified
model. They dive into research around and about the topic or
problem at hand. Immersion into the site—including the history, art, literature, philosophy, geography, and language of the
site's culture—gives them a marinade in which to simmer while
they wait for ideas to come to them. Ingels takes *in* impressions
of the world, instead of stamping impressions of the world *out*.
There is no Platonic ideal fixed still in time and space, perfect

in its universality. Ingels designs dynamically, in constant conversation with the fluid realities—political, environmental, economic, social—of the site itself. By staying open to more diverse sets of data, he is able to reinvent what a building could and should look like in response to the circumstances, or what he calls "the set of criteria."

One of BIG's earliest designs was a series of housing projects outside Copenhagen. Embarking on the project, Ingels found the conventions of housing-project architecture to be stultifying, and he knew he had to find a better way of addressing the needs of the residents. "There is a very limited set of criteria in a housing project: something about the daylight orientation and the minimum distance from one house to the next and that's about it. There is nothing about the diversity of households, what happens between the buildings, climatic diversity, interconnectedness, shelter from the rain and wind."

These early housing projects helped Ingels understand that the only way to escape standard solutions was to embrace the criteria. Instead of railing against the limitations—whether from clients or context—he began adding on more limitations particular to the site. You might smile when I tell you that— no coincidence—one of his favorite games is Twister. Much like his buildings, participants in Twister start out looking "normal," standing up straight and tall with both feet on the ground. But then, bit by bit, as the game progresses, the players are forced to bend, twist, and double over. His buildings, like the Twister players, look the way they do because it is the only way to elegantly solve the problems set before them in the game.

This process of integrating many types of input, many types of data, makes BIG unique in the architectural world. Their architecture is driven not by aesthetics per se but by an understanding that synthesizes all aspects of the site: the economics, financials, planning people, historical cultures, restrictions, and environmental issues. "Rather than trying to solve everything from an aesthetic point of view, we use constraints as an invitation to create a surprise or change the design. You can end up refining the design not by adding ornament but by adding performance."

Consider the way BIG achieved a creative breakthrough in their designs for an ethnographic museum in a major park in Budapest: "We wanted the museum to be 'Budapest-esque' so we spent some time there—we went to the bathhouses. It was ten in the evening in the winter and we were swimming outside in these warm baths underneath the winter sky. The city is East and West and borderline Middle East and borderline Russia and the Eastern Roman Empire. There is a certain heaviness there."

Note the way Ingels uses phenomenology to describe the city ("a certain heaviness…") and the experience of the bathhouses in the winter. This gets synthesized into his team's open-ended inquiry of the practical and aesthetic possibilities of the site: "It is on the axis of this long, long boulevard and it arrives at a major park. The master plan dictated some kind of gate-like structure so that was where we started, but what did a gate have to do with the building as an ethnographic museum and a building projecting the culture of Hungary to the world?"

The team worked with designs of a gate using historical

vernacular from the Roman baths as well as ceramic tiles on the façade but, as Ingels put it, "There was nothing at the core. We were looking at all these little models but there was still something that did not make sense. You want the gate to be grand but then of course, once you approach it, it also wants to be inviting."

BIG kept navigating around the challenge of a gate and a monument that would also function as an ethnographic museum. The design needed to embody the tension between something opaque—monumental—and something more transparent and accessible: the living history of Hungary.

"Finally," Ingels told me, "I said, maybe we slice the gate open? So you see a perfect monolithic material that becomes this beautiful gate. But then when you pass through it, like a tunnel, you realize there are layers. And these layers, the walls of the tunnel, display the ethnographic collection. So as you pass through, you are actually looking into the museum."

By showcasing the entirety of the museum's collection behind the glass vitrines in the walls, visitors could walk through the gate and see all of the archives on display. It would be a glimpse into the richness of the collection—a snapshot of Hungary's history.

"From the park," Ingels explained, "200 meters down the avenue, you see this beautiful Arc de Triomphe, except that there is something off about it because it rounds at the bottom. And then, once you get closer, you realize that the monument is transforming into something human-scale. It is inviting visitors to pass through the museum and see the collection en masse."

The moment the BIG team saw the idea in its execution on

the computer, the mood in the room shifted. There was sharp intake of air and then spontaneous cheers and high fives. "It was just so clear to everyone on the team that this was going to be amazing," Ingels told me.

He likened this experience with creative breakthrough to a moment of walking through a managed forest. From a distance, you see nothing but chaos—the trees are clumped together in seemingly random assortments. And then, suddenly, when the insight hits—bam—everything snaps into shape and all the trees are lined up in perfect rows. "We had been circling toward it and it felt right but it didn't make any sense. And then, with the right idea, suddenly the concept, the program, the park in the city...everything makes sense."

If this type of abductive reasoning has a pitfall, it is the false signposts, the descent into intuition alone. Ingels, like George Soros, Robert Johnson, and the other masters we will meet in the next chapter, never stops changing perspectives. He never allows his ideas to become static or assumes a linear progression to the process.

"We look at ideas in 3-D in the model; we look at it in the planned section, we evaluate the section, the projection, the physical model. Then we evaluate the square meters—like how does it actually accommodate the program. Each time, we change perspective and look at it with a different set of eyes. And each time we change the perspective, we've found a new thing that you need to fix."

"This frustration that you've been feeling....You know there is something there....And then suddenly, it's almost like..." Ingels made a sound to capture the experience of an insight arriving: *Click click click click.* "I don't mean it's like a checklist, but you just feel that it works on all levels and this new idea.... As if all these types of data meet in a shape. Or in a construct." He landed on just the right phrase: "It's an inarguable truth."

The click: This is grace.

Chapter Seven

The North Star—Not the GPS

Everything you're sure is right can be wrong in another place.

—*Barbara Kingsolver,* The Poisonwood Bible

In the late nineties, the U.S. Naval Academy did away with its coursework on celestial navigation and replaced it all with training based on GPS and satellite technology. In the wake of hacking threats, however, the academy has reversed this decision. In 2015, they announced that they would, once again, require officers in the navy to have a working knowledge of navigation by the stars. Frank Reed, an expert in celestial navigation, told WBUR's *Here & Now* that a return to this older form of navigation was not about the romance of an ancient practice. "Every navigator," he said, "should use *all* the available information." In this way, navigation is less about blindly following the GPS or a satellite and much more about assembling an interpretation from all forms of data.

Celestial navigation provides an apt metaphor for leadership in today's organizations and companies. Instead of simply *reacting* to one type of data, it is the role of the leader to make sense of *all* data: to interpret the facts available from multiple sources—technical and human—and to develop a strategy accordingly.

In this chapter, I want to introduce you to several sense-makers who have cultivated mastery in this interpretive art. The skills they possess could never be captured in any kind of quantitative evaluation. As a result, this kind of intelligence—extraordinary in its sensitivity, sophistication, and courage—often goes unheralded. And yet, if the hardest—and most lucrative—problems of the coming century are *cultural*, then these are the very skills we need to be celebrating. In the following four stories, we encounter expertise in social intuition, political innovation, active listening, cultural interpretation, analytical empathy, and artistic integrity. Here is sensemaking as it is practiced by everyday masters:

1. Sheila Heen: Becoming One with the Room

I am always assessing and responding to the core emotional interests in the room.

Sheila Heen is a master teacher in the negotiation and conflict resolution field. She and her colleagues have been team-teaching an advanced class called Difficult Conversations at Harvard Law School for twenty years now. Through her consulting firm, Triad Consulting, she and her partners also work with corporate clients and organizations to equip leaders to address the hornet's nest of issues that come up around conflict, influence, and leadership in the workplace.

At a recent session with a Fortune 500 corporation, Heen stood in front of a room filled with people from different departments in the company. She was there to do a session on "feedback": working with senior leaders to build their capacity to give and receive feedback in more productive ways. As they talked about the challenges and dilemmas feedback presents, one particularly outspoken executive raised his hand and offered, "I have problems with the way my wife gives me feedback."

His colleagues chuckled.

"She won't just tell me what she wants," he told the room. "Her feedback is incredibly unclear."

Heen's job in moments like these—to help these leaders learn about themselves and about communication—is complicated. She knows that everyone in the room is a senior executive—she has the org chart that lays out the official roles and hierarchy of the leaders in the room. But more important than the job titles are the relationships in the room among the executives and how they perceive each other: Who is respected? Whose advice or insight carries weight? Who is seen as "difficult"? Who is trusted? Who is beloved?

Heen knew instantly that the man was well-liked. She could feel that from the mood in the room and the warmth of the laughter. But she could also see from the half smiles on people's faces that the executive didn't always have clarity on how others perceived him.

"So what do you say to her when that happens?" Heen asked in response. She could feel the curiosity in the room open up even more, as those assembled were interested in what they might learn if she pressed their colleague further.

And he was eager to share more. "I say, 'I don't understand what you want from me.'" He raised his palms in defiance, offering up a gesture of frustration to the room. "Come back to me when you know what you want me to do," he concluded.

Heen didn't miss a beat, "So you're telling her that you only want feedback from her when it's perfectly articulated."

"Yes," the executive said with satisfaction. "Exactly."

At this point, the room shot up in temperature. Recognition swelled like a wave, moving from one participant to another, gathering force. An insight was breaking. Heen now had a decision of insurmountable complexity in front of her: how best to ride this wave of insight to maximize the learning while also managing the risks involved. The room was starting to understand the man's blind spot about protecting himself from receiving feedback, although he himself did not. Should she expose him in front of the others, explicitly drawing out the insight and using it as a way to break open the workshop? Or should she end the conversation and hope that this executive and everyone else would reflect back on the moment and arrive at some kind of understanding later on? Exposing him would offer up a wealth of pedagogical riches, but what if it caused him shame or embarrassment? What if he became angry or sullen and this soured the open and trusting atmosphere of the workshop she had established?

Countless different data streams go into every single millisecond of Heen's craft. Beyond the org chart she is always reading (and re-reading); there is the real-time social context of each and every executive she is addressing in the moment. But there is a second aspect to relationships that she is also always reading: the leaders' relationship with themselves. Are they self-conscious? How much do they care about others' opinions, or looking good to their peers? Do they want to be here?

Are they cynical? If they have a sudden—and public—aha moment, will they find it exhilarating or humiliating? Most importantly, do they have a sense of humor about themselves?

Every single clue she extracts about an individual can dynamically change as the room shifts from mood to mood. One individual might be reticent at first but then become gregarious and fun-loving when the mood of the room shifts over to jovial and playful. Another individual might begin with a very impassive response and then grow more aggressive or more deferential depending on the feedback from her superiors or someone she respects nearby.

But all of that is just the beginning. Heen also has to know about the company culture as a whole. Do they perceive of themselves as competitive? Egalitarian? Creative? Hard-nosed? The underdogs? The alphas? The only ones who "get it" but are still treated as second-class citizens as a team or function? Once she has an understanding of the larger picture, Heen then needs to sense the chafing points within that culture. Where do the misunderstandings occur? How are aspects of the culture holding certain people and departments back? What can be said out loud and what remains unspoken? How much can Heen push any one individual in any given moment and how much can she push them as a group?

All of these considerations have not even touched upon her material. It is a given that Heen knows her content cold—just as the jazz musician shows up at the club with a technical expertise—but she has to use that content to tune in to the students. She has to reach outside herself to make something magic happen in the room.

As the room grew hushed, Heen knew just what to do. "It

sounds like you only want perfectly delivered feedback," she shot back at him with a playful smile.

The room tittered in growing anticipation.

"Well," the executive considered this. "I guess that's true..."

"But can feedback ever really be *perfectly* delivered?" She paused, gauging his facial expression as he followed her reasoning, then added, "It's kind of a clever way to ensure she can never actually give you feedback, no?" she teased.

The man stood still, shocked, momentarily off balance. The room erupted in laughter and then he, too, smiled; his entire demeanor suddenly cracked open with a new understanding about himself and his relationships.

"Yeah," he said, laughing at himself along with the room. "Yeah, I guess feedback can't ever be *perfect*."

"I *still* make this mistake," Heen confided to the room, deftly shifting the focus away from the man and back onto her teaching. "I feel really frustrated when people offer me unclear or unfair or poorly delivered feedback. But giving and receiving feedback is not about finding the perfect words, or even the *right words*. It's really about having the *right attitude*. If we want to receive feedback well, we need to be curious about what someone is trying to tell us—even when they are doing a terrible job of telling us. We're usually going to have to work to see what our givers are trying to say."

In that moment, the tension broke. The room, as if a single entity, absorbed Heen's insight. Teacher and students: everyone was "in it" together. Over lunch the executive approached Heen to thank her and tell her how "big" that learning was for him, both for his marriage, and also for his leadership.

"The research I present on how to deliver feedback and

have difficult conversations melds with the way I interact with them as a teacher," Heen told me later that day. "The teaching itself is a negotiation. You're negotiating for engagement and credibility, a willingness to try new things and to own up to mistakes without getting defensive. I have to be using the skills I'm teaching in how I'm teaching them."

Whether teaching or mediating complex conflicts, Heen described her overall experience with reading all of the complex human signals as "crossing over the river."

"There are moments when my internal voice is preoccupied with the content—how to explain something more clearly or what to say next—but then, inevitably, I cross over the river and the material is at my fingertips. Then my internal voice is completely focused on the people in the room and reading all those signals that help me help them learn or move forward. When I am speaking from inside the content, I can respond in the moment to the context. Then it's all happening in real time."

2. Margrethe Vestager: Reading between the Rules

It's dangerous to just enforce rules without an understanding of consequences and opportunities.

In 2014, Margrethe Vestager was appointed the European Commissioner for Competition, head of the European Union's antitrust agency. She received a flurry of press in 2015 for taking on Google in Europe and Gazprom, Russia's state-owned gas behemoth. Though Vestager is an experienced politician after twenty-eight years in Danish politics, she is anything but a bureaucrat.

"In a bureaucratic system, data is very abstract—mostly numbers and reports," she told me. "The data is well done technically, but it is very hard to get any feel for what kind of human situation underlies the documents. What is really going on for people?"

She sees her work as a constant dance between generalities and specifics. The EU—and her role in particular—is constructed around enforcing rules. But without a granular understanding of the particularities in each and every situation, she is at risk of making huge mistakes.

"The system is set up to deal with things in general ways, but I need to make sure we counterbalance that," she explained. "That's why I never make any decisions solely based on, say, economic data. I need to feel it too. I don't see this as an irrational process. I see it as a helpful way to circle around something and perhaps understand with my gut and my humanity as well as with my head."

Vestager recently started to investigate Italian state support for the steel producer Ilva. With funding from the government, Ilva was able to revamp its steel plant in Taranto, Italy. This public support allowed the steel company—the EU's largest—to optimize its resources: projections put the Taranto factory's future production on par with the steel industries of Bulgaria, Greece, Hungary, Croatia, Slovenia, Romania, and Luxembourg *combined* in 2015.

Considering Europe's recent job losses in the steel industry as a result of the glut of cheap Chinese steel on the markets, Vestager's call seems straightforward: Italy's state support of Ilva is against the rules of free competition. It's an open-and-shut case.

For Vestager, however, judgments are never either/or. She works within a continuum, envisioning her role of enforcer as more of a barometer of ever-shifting political dynamics. "If you close down a plant with fifteen thousand people, you impact the whole area," she told me. "If you don't have an understanding of the people, the area, and, most important, the capacity for the area to change, you might end up decimating the area's economy. It's dangerous to just enforce rules without this understanding of consequences and opportunities."

Vestager relates to these rules the way great chefs relate to recipes. Instead of rigidly clinging to her mandate, she exercises something much more fluid. Her judgment transcends the abstract guidelines as she fully immerses herself in each and every specific context. She is able to do this, in part, because she has so many decades of experience in the political arena, where alliances and constituencies are constantly shifting. But she also utilizes analytical empathy to better understand worlds like the one in Taranto, Italy.

"The best way for me to connect to people is to be amidst them, feeling what they do and what they can do. But the second best way to connect is to read their fiction. I can understand what it feels like to be a young immigrant when I read fiction about growing up in the outskirts of Paris. And there is excellent fiction out there exploring the experience of Albanian refugees in Italy. It doesn't matter that these are works of fiction and hence less scientific than the numbers and reports. They describe a human experience and that is what makes them true."

The challenge for Vestager is to stay vigilant about gathering this type of data in the midst of the bureaucratic culture in Brussels. "Because of my job," she said, "I am protected against reality. It really shouldn't be that way. I should be deeply embedded in reality."

In an effort to dismantle some of the mechanisms of bureaucracy, she made immediate changes to the layout of her new offices when she arrived in Brussels. Not only was she surrounded by layers of assistants and aides—blocking out the real-world knowledge she needed to serve her electorate—the very placement of her work desk was keeping her at a distance from her work.

"There is a table—a huge one—between me and them. This is the language of power. But the problem is twofold: I don't get any feel for what people do, want, or need because my sensitivity is blocked, and they don't need to take responsibility for what they say, because they are put in a situation where we are not equals."

Vestager refers to this as the "gulf of veneer": the distance bureaucracy puts between people with differing positions of power. She moved her desk sideways so that she was immediately in direct contact with her visitors, diffusing the dynamic. Now she gets full access to them and they get full access to her.

"In a way it is much tougher on them. If they talk to me and they feel they are equal to me, they also need to take responsibility for what they are saying. I am naturally the one with the ultimate responsibility and I accept that, but if we are two people talking to one another on equal terms, what they say can't be hidden between anything."

As Vestager works to build the EU's case against tech giants like Google—first arguing that their search business was artificially excluding rivals and now going after Google's mobile operating systems—she is always taking the temperature of the governing bodies around her as well as of the culture at large. In this way, she is immersed in the whole of the political system; she feels it as a part of her body.

"When the ministry or the people affected aren't ready, it feels like my muscles are tense. If it is the right time to do something, however, I feel like I am standing on a beach looking out on the ocean. Total openness and completely at ease. It sounds strange, but it is crucial to success that you are open to feeling at one with the people you deal with. You must empathize with their life and concerns. That means you really must walk in their shoes."

3. Chris Voss: Understanding the Antagonistic World

We had to acknowledge their culture to transform the relationship from a manipulation to a collaboration.

On January 7, 2006, a young American journalist named Jill Carroll was kidnapped in the Adel district of Baghdad after being ambushed by masked gunmen. Carroll's driver managed to escape, but her interpreter was shot dead on site and then abandoned. News of Carroll's kidnapping—the thirty-first such attack on foreign journalists during the war with Iraq—was met with international alarm and an outpouring of support.

Nothing was heard from Carroll for close to two weeks and then, on January 17, Al Jazeera showed a video featuring her.

Jill Carroll's voice had been edited out, her head was uncovered and her hair disheveled, and there were two men all in
black with masked faces standing on either side of her holding
guns. A third man was standing directly behind her—also in
black with a masked face—holding a book above her head. The
video demanded that all the women in Iraqi jails be released
within 72 hours, or Carroll would face immediate execution.

In a moment of crisis like this, the FBI calls upon a team
of highly skilled negotiators to navigate the next steps. Chris
Voss, an FBI agent for more than two decades, was the lead
international kidnapping negotiator in the FBI's crisis negotiation unit. He remembers the moment he saw the first released
video of Carroll. Because of his years of training, he was immediately able to decode its message.

"When the case started, it looked really bad," he told me.
"In that video, it was clear that they had already passed judgment on her. The guy is standing behind her with a book, and
that is communicating that she has been tried and convicted by
a higher power. They are framing this not as a murder, but as a
justified execution by a state."

As in all of Voss's negotiations, his first priority in the Carroll case was to determine who, exactly, is negotiating with
whom. He described the kidnappers' demand as a setup because
there was no realistic way for the Americans—or anyone—to
assess how many women were in the Iraqi jails, much less determine whether they might be freed in a matter of only days. The
audacity of the request was the first warning sign to Voss that
the kidnappers were not, in fact, negotiating with anyone in
the West.

"We are not the audience for that video. They are speaking

to the undecided in the Middle East. Because of that, our next step had to be a way of communicating that resonated with that same group of people."

In this type of delicate negotiation—orchestrated primarily through the theater of the media—many of the challenges revolve around effectively coaching family members in the messages delivered to the press. These messages are then broadcast out across the world.

"By the time we worked on the Carroll case," Voss explained to me, "we had come to develop an understanding of the cultural themes that mattered most to these insurgents in Iraq. We had to acknowledge their culture if we had any hope of transforming the relationship from a manipulation to a collaboration."

For Voss, this transformation always begins and ends with active listening; he calls it our most underutilized tool in solving complex social problems. But active listening is only possible when we engage with a particular kind of empathy. We can liken this to the analytical empathy I described in Chapter Four.

"It's almost easier to say what this type of empathy is not: It's not about being nice; it's not about agreeing; it's not about *liking* the other side. It is just straight observation and then an articulation of what you see. I can be empathic with Jihadi John, a terrorist executioner. It doesn't have anything to do with approving of his actions."

Using his experience with previous cases and his well-developed skills with this type of negotiation, Voss worked with his team to meticulously craft the right message. This approach involved sending out messages to everyone in contact with the media—including family members and politicians.

"When anyone asked us about the Jill Carroll case, we would say, 'Did you see how they disrespected her by leaving her head uncovered? They broke their own rules.' And then politicians, media, family, they would all say: 'Yeah. You're right.' And then they would repeat this same idea about disrespect in all of their media appearances. We can't explain our message *to* them. They have to discover it *through* us so they can repeat it with their full emotional investment."

That media manipulation was one step in a multipronged strategy. Simultaneously, Voss's team was working with Jill Carroll's family and coaching them on their talking points.

"Any effective negotiation always needs to begin by expressing an inarguable truth. With an inarguable truth, no one can disagree no matter what side they are on. People always want to say, 'She's innocent,' or 'They shouldn't have kidnapped her.' These messages in the media are counterproductive. They are only speaking to *us*. We needed to speak to the undecided in the Middle East."

Several members of the Carroll family—including her mother and sister—were not fully convinced of the merits of such a strict script. They wanted to express their fury, fear, and sadness in their own words. Jim Carroll, Jill Carroll's dad, however, agreed. Voss knew that using Jim Carroll as the messenger would be a cue of respect to the insurgents because in Middle Eastern cultures, all honor flows through the father. He arranged for an exclusive media agreement with CNN where a cameraman could film Jim Carroll stating only his script, with no other interview questions or analysis. This video would then be sent directly to Al Jazeera.

"We coached Jill Carroll's dad on the entire approach. We

started with an inarguable truth: 'Jill Carroll is not your enemy.' From there, we continued to make an appeal to the viewers in the Middle East. 'Jill Carroll had been reporting on the plight of the Iraqi people.' And then finally Jim Carroll said, 'When you let her go, she will go back to doing the same reporting.'"

The video went out unedited to Middle Eastern media sources. Although Voss and his team had no influence over when and where it aired, they had confidence that the insurgents would see it at some point. It was only later, upon Jill Carroll's release, that Voss learned that Jim Carroll's words played a powerful role in her release.

"Jill Carroll told us that when her kidnappers saw her father on Al Jazeera, they said: 'Your father is an honorable man.' In the Middle East, if someone says your father is an honorable man, *bang.* There is a shield of honor around you and everyone in your family. The very next video that they released with her a few weeks later, she is by herself and her hair is covered with a headscarf."

A third and final video was released on February 9, 2006. In it, Jill Carroll sits in full Islamic dress. She continues to plead for support with her release, but her voice is included in the video and she sits alone with no armed men standing around her.

"In the third video, there was no sense of a threat," Voss explained. "It was clear to me that these guys were just trying to figure out how to let her go and save face. She was calm and she looked very well taken care of. They have one hundred percent control of the content, so when we saw that video, we knew she was safe."

On March 30 of that same year, Jill Carroll was officially

released. She walked into the Sunni Iraqi Islamic Party offices in Baghdad and told officials there that she had been freed unharmed after being cared for and treated humanely during her more than sixty days in captivity.

Voss's particular skill set synthesized an acute emotional intelligence with his experience and knowledge of the Middle Eastern culture. His success with the Jill Carroll case would not have been possible without either of those strengths. "I like to define negotiation as emotional intelligence on steroids," Voss said. "The key to success is navigating the other person's emotions. In a hostage situation, emotions might seem to be larger than normal, but it doesn't mean they're any different."

Through his interpretive skills as a negotiator, he approached a high-stakes situation with an understanding of narrative and messaging in several different contexts: his own, the context of the American media, the context of the kidnappers, and, finally, the context of the Middle Eastern population watching the unfolding drama. He played each and every context as part of his greater orchestration: the goal of a securing a release for Carroll.

"We used to say the most dangerous negotiation is the one you don't know you're in. Who is a terrorist's target by threatening an American on film? They don't care how Americans respond. They are thinking about Jihadi John, who is now a heartthrob. They have miscreants around the globe who want to be Jihadi John. They all want to join up."

Although there were several other media and political efforts around the globe advocating for Jill Carroll—each one a factor in her ultimate release—Carroll reported that her captors started treating her differently immediately after the video of her father was shown on TV.

"One of the most effective weapons against terrorism is the truth," Voss stated. "The truth was that Jill Carroll was not the enemy of her captors. Her father spoke that truth, and the rest of the world repeated it."

Becoming a Connoisseur

Sheila Heen, Margrethe Vestager, and Chris Voss have all found a way to successfully navigate their worlds with interpretative skills. To help us to understand this better, I offer up a word often associated with the fine arts or culinary endeavors: connoisseur. For our sensemaking journey, I would like to return the word to its French origins: the verb *connaître* means "to be acquainted with" or "to know somebody/a place." Mastery—*connaissance*—is a way of navigating through a body of knowledge.

The further we go into our chosen endeavors—whether they be teaching, hostage negotiation, or politics—the more we can categorize our knowledge. Consider techniques for cooking meat. In the United States we recognize five stages, beginning with *rare* and ending with *well-done*. In France, however, the culture of meat and cooking is much richer. French chefs must navigate among nine different categories, beginning with *bleu*—a steak that has lightly touched a hot pan, remaining completely raw inside—all the way up to *carbonisé*, or extremely well-done and even leathery on the outside. There is a very important spot between rare and medium rare in French cooking—*à point*—that one cannot ask for in the United States. As we add more experience to our sensemaking, we discover more analytical categories. This is the process of becoming a connoisseur: it is a way of navigating through the world.

Recall Sheila Heen: her journey is characterized by an ever-increasing knowledge of the atmosphere of her students in the room. She is now able to recognize many more moods in her classroom and, as a result, she can navigate successfully toward her teaching moments. If the room is cold and quiet, filled with tired or withdrawn faces, she knows to add in some humor and playfulness. If, on the other hand, it is a room filled with defiance and anger—managers who don't really want to be in attendance—she finds a way to align her interests with theirs. She puts herself on the same team with them and encourages them to confide their frustrations in her.

"Early on I would be attached to my notes and I was putting all my attention on how to explain the content to my students. After years and years of working with groups, I felt confident enough in the material to let the teaching come more automatically, and I could tune into the room. I could see so much more on the faces of the students. Who was paying attention and who was not, who was open to engagement with humor and who was more reticent."

As her teaching reached a level of mastery, these analytical categories of social acuity increased even more. Heen was able to recognize not only the dynamics that existed between her and each individual student but the different relationships between the students themselves. Earlier in her career, she might have recognized someone as the leader, and another group of people as managers under that leader. Over time, these categories exploded into dozens and even hundreds of different ways of categorizing the relationship to the hierarchy within the room. Heen became a connoisseur of human relationships and social moods.

She described a moment when she was teaching to a room filled with high-powered bankers in London. "Everyone was important and there was not a lot of pecking order to the room. For that very reason, I knew I could use status and have some fun with it as a teaching tool. When I forgot to address a table in the back, I made a joke and called it the 'remedial table.' The entire room lit up with laughter and goodwill. It was just the right thing to say to twenty-five of the most powerful people in banking. It opened all of us up to learn from each other."

For Margrethe Vestager, the EU commissioner, sensemaking knowledge is characterized by an increasing sensitivity to different rhythms within the whole of the political system. After two decades in politics, she can now see opportunities for possible reforms that others cannot see. And, by the same token, she also knows when she can't move something forward.

"*When* to do something is as important as what to do," she explained to me. "The window to launch a new initiative or a political program is often so small. I feel my way to understand this. Are people ready for this? Can they take more change now? What emotional state will people be in when we do this?"

And Chris Voss, the negotiator, has learned to navigate through the varying emotional registers in other people's voices. His listening skills guide him in assessing when there is openness for possible collaboration. "When you begin to get an ear for the positives and negatives implied in the conversation, you can specifically choose to reinforce the positives and diminish the negatives," he said. "And although it might not be enough, you can always lean into it in some way. It definitely takes practice and it is absolutely a perishable skill."

On all of these journeys, the siren song is that there will be a model or a theory of everything that will organize all of the various factors under one framework: the GPS to plug in or a satellite to provide guidance through the dark. The true connoisseur, however, understands that there is no one right answer. Navigation is not about paying attention to everything. It is about artfully interpreting something.

Heen pays more attention to the role that hierarchy plays in her teaching. When she enters a room, she is able to sense how her own status will be received and how to either diffuse that status or elevate it in order to gain traction for a better learning environment.

Vestager needs to know the secondary and tertiary consequences of her political actions. To do this, she has developed her knowledge of the EU's system of governance as if it is an intimate friend. She can get a read on a new system she encounters and know if it is stressed out, excited, hopeful, or despondent. This knowledge guides her decisions about what types of changes are possible.

Voss is keenly aware of the nuances of manipulation. Whether he is in an investigation or a barricade situation or a kidnapping negotiation, he is always looking for windows of opportunity to shift manipulation into collaboration. He excels at getting people to talk to him without using leverage, or threatening force.

In this way, all three of these masters have cultivated a perspective from within their given craft. And it is this perspective that ultimately leads to the most defining aspect of connoisseurship: aesthetic judgment. This is where navigation becomes an interpretive art. In both the sciences *and* humanist endeavors, there are many possible roads to the same destination. Which one is the most beautiful? The most compelling? The most powerful? The most pleasing? An algorithm can arrive at optimization, but only a human being—an artist, a thinker, a mathematician, an entrepreneur, a politician—only someone with a sense of perspective can interpret the meaning of the destination. Masters spend their entire lives in pursuit of this interpretation. This is how they make sense of the world.

The Alchemy of Sensemaking

Just off Route 29 in California's Napa Valley, a gray barn with the clean architectural lines of another era stands watch over several acres of St. George rootstock vineyards. A knotted rope swing hangs in front of the property, and one lone Prius is parked in the small lot. This is the Corison Winery, home to the venerable Cathy Corison, a winemaker who has been making Napa Valley Cabernet on her own terms for close to forty years.

Though the interior of the barn is humble—there is no formal tasting room, and picnic tables holding wine bottles and glasses sit side by side with wine tanks and wood barrels—Corison exudes a quiet power when she comes out to meet me. Now in her early sixties, Corison has earned her stripes in the Napa Valley community. After graduating with a master's degree in enology from the University of California at Davis, the country's preeminent wine studies program, she started working in the Napa Valley.

In the years following Prohibition, the wine industry in the Napa Valley consisted of a few sleepy vineyards and a lot of sweet wine. The modern wine industry as we know it began to emerge in the mid-1960s, supported by research done at the University of California. Then, in 1976—right after Corison showed up in Napa—the wine world, dominated by the French, was stunned when California's wines bested their French counterparts in a blind tasting with French wine critics. Napa Valley became a hotbed of activity with the emergence of new wines and new ways of making wine. Unlike the traditional European vineyards, American winemakers fully embraced technology like cold fermentation: by placing the grapes in a stainless steel vat with double walls, the winemakers were able to pass a coolant through them to control the fermentation, leading to fresher and crisper American white wines.

Corison came of age when these types of new technologies were emerging. She and her fellow UC Davis graduates initially approached winemaking through the lens of their technical training, holding the older growers in disdain for their lack of scientific knowledge. Now, four decades later, Corison sees things differently. "There was a lot of wisdom from the old-timers. We were full of ourselves, but the more you know the less you know."

By the late 1980s, Corison had been making wine for the famous label Chappellet for close to a decade. The vineyards of Chappellet, up in the hills of Napa Valley, had gone through a few seasons of drought, so Corison and her team sourced some additional grapes from down on the Rutherford Bench. This "bench" is made up of well-drained alluvial soils, unlike the rocky terrain up in the hills. Most important, the bench is gravelly loam—composed of roughly equal parts of sand, silt, and clay—so it has great water-holding capacity but excellent drainage. Vines in loam soil get the water they need to grow in the spring and summer. Gravel makes the soil well-drained so when the rains stop coming, the vines stop growing and focus on ripening.

"If Cabernet is growing when it ought to be ripening its fruit, it maintains green flavors," Corison explained. Ripeness in Cabernet Sauvignon is marked by the evolution of red, blue, purple, and black fruit flavors and the disappearance of green notes. "If the vine stops growing and gets busy ripening, however, there is a chance to get grapes fully ripe without the sugars getting too high."

When Corison and her crew began sourcing grapes from these alluvial loam soils, she had a revelation about the kind of wine she wanted to make. "There was a wine inside me that needed to get out," Corison told me. "That's the only way I can describe it. It was both powerful and elegant. Cabernet is going to be powerful no matter what you do, but it's way more interesting to me at the intersection of elegance. When we sourced grapes from down in the valley, I learned that this wine that needed to get out grows on the Rutherford Bench."

Starting in 1987, Corison embraced this vision and began making her own wines. She found wineries with excess capacity and used their facilities to create her Napa Valley Cabernet. In 1995, she and her husband bought a small plot of land that runs from Rutherford to St. Helena. Everyone else had turned down the land because they assumed that the vines would need to be replanted and the old property on it torn down. Corison and her husband forged ahead, turning the derelict property into a barn to house their facility. And they did not replant the old vines on St. George rootstock. Instead, they celebrated them.

"Those vines are just wise—they are old and wise. I think it has to do with root depth. They come through heat spells with grace and style when all the younger vineyards are really hurting. They know what to do."

During this time, the fashion in Napa Valley was big and bold. New World winemakers in California tended to let the fruit sit longer on the vine for powerful aromas and flavors. The alcohol levels of these wines began to stretch well above 14 percent. Some critics lauded them as "lush," while others derisively referred to them as "fruit bombs." In the late 1980s and early 90's Napa Valley looked less and less like an agricultural community and more and more like a playground for the rich and famous. The lushness of the wines reflected the grandiosity of these drinkers.

The "numbers" of these more robust wines were all scientifically correct. The wines were all technically sound, with structural integrity. The winemakers could clearly state the properties of their "ripe" wines: the sugar, acid, and pH levels of the grapes all measured in an appropriate range.

The aspects of ripeness, however, tell a much more nuanced story. "Ripeness happens at different numbers every year," Corison explained. "If you are not out in the vineyard, seeing it, you don't really know. Numbers are just a piece of it. The vines get tired by the end of the ripening season and can give up after a while. And when they give up, true ripening ends. That is the challenge: to make all the components converge at just the right time. A great vintage is when all those factors converge right where you want them. It's biology and chemistry, but also alchemy. There is so much we don't understand on a technical level."

Care

Every single word Corison uses to articulate her wine and her winemaking conveys her relationship to the land. These vines are not measured in scientific properties: the pH, salinity, and lime content of their soil suitability, for example. Instead, she describes them as "old and wise," with "grace and style."

"We have all the heat and sunshine we need to get the grapes right—even in a cold season like 2011—but because of the cold nights and the fog coming in, we have beautiful natural acidity too. And the tannins in [this] corner of the world come in feeling like velvet. If you were to measure the tannins, you'd get a very big number. But tannins are not one molecule; they're a class of molecules that can range from harsh and astringent to soft and velvety and beautiful. And that is what I love about benchland fruit: there are fruit flavors, but the tannins are so luscious. They feel good."

Corison could never gain this type of perspective from a spreadsheet or an office on the 87th floor of a skyscraper. She knows the tannins feel like velvet because she has been tasting them for close to forty years. Ultimately, she can hold this aesthetic judgment because of how specifically she is situated in her context. To put it simply, Cathy Corison gives a damn: "I cut my teeth on European wines. And I tasted enough of the old Cabernets from that neck of the woods to know elegance. It's a moral imperative for me to make a wine that will be long-lived and do interesting things in the bottle."

When you have a perspective—when you actually give a damn—you intuitively sense what's important and what's trivial. You can see what connects with what, and you know the data, input, and knowledge that matter. Caring is the connective tissue that makes all these things possible.

Conversely, a *lack* of care is often at the root of many of the business and organizational challenges I encounter in my consulting. Over time, as management has become increasingly professionalized, you can sense a kind of nihilism or loss of meaning in the executive layers. This nihilism is strongest in large corporate cultures where management is seen as a profession in and of itself, with no strong connection to what the company actually makes or does. What happens when satisfaction in work comes from managing—reorganizing, optimizing the operation, hiring new people, and making strategies—and not from producing something meaningful? How do you feel when it doesn't really matter whether you make beauty products, soft drinks, fast food, or musical instruments?

Without care, everything is "correct" and nothing is "true." Martin Heidegger claimed that care—or what he called *Sorge*—is the very thing that makes us human. He didn't mean "care" as an explicit emotional connection with things or people, but rather in the sense that something matters to you, is meaningful to you. It is this care that enables us to interact with stuff in very complex ways, and it is also this care that enables us to see new ways of interacting with the world.

If you are in the beauty business, you simply can't make sense of cultural insights regarding beauty ideals if you don't care about the meaning of beauty products. If you are in the car industry, you have to care about cars and transportation—otherwise, the human phenomenon of driving will not make sense to you. Without care, you stop seeing the bigger picture of meaning and insight and you only see discrete data points—what Isaiah Berlin referred to as "so many individual butterflies."

Care is what allowed Cathy Corison to hear the call of the wine trying to "get out" of her. And care is what gives her the courage to continue to make it, year after year after year. Today it is in fashion. Ten years ago, it was not. Care provides her with a North Star so she doesn't get distracted or waylaid throughout these cycles of wine and culinary fashion.

Consider Leo McCloskey, founder of a wine consulting group called Enologix. Whereas Cathy Corison's wine is never just about the numbers, McCloskey has developed an entire business model around the belief that winemaking is *all* about numbers. With the world's largest wine database, he tastes hundreds of wines a year and then breaks all of them down into the individual compounds that give them their unique color, flavor, and fragrance.

What does he do with all this information? He begins by running computer tests for his clients to help determine the most important moment of the season: when to pick the grapes. This reverse-engineers the wines, stripping them down to their component parts and atomizing each and every element. These results get compared with his vast database—calculated along with captured data about conditions in the vineyard, such as the rainfall and water levels and winemaking process details like the types of barrels used and the length of fermentation. All of these models give winemakers a way to create virtual versions of their wine: playing with different factors to tweak particular elements, akin to creating a Fantasy Football League.

When the wine is ready to go in the bottle, Enologix has one final offering: their calculations can predict with a fair amount of accuracy how the wine will score on the infamous 100-point scale in *Wine Spectator*.

It's a *Moneyball* approach to winemaking, an audacious move in a culture that holds firmly to its identity as an artisanal craft. McCloskey does not reveal the names of his clients, but he primarily serves the smaller vineyards attempting to stay close to the traditional methods of winemaking made famous in Old World cultures like Burgundy and Alsace. These clients, and several sources in the industry, believe that McCloskey has something valuable to offer winemakers. But anyone who spends time with Cathy Corison knows that this value is a mirage. Nothing in McCloskey's "black box" has any lasting point of view. By taking an entirely objective approach to the data—and treating the compounds in a bottle of wine as atomized elements discrete from their greater context—McCloskey has every chance of helping to make good wine today. But he will never come close to making great wine that endures. This is because there is no integrity, no aesthetic—there is no person who cares—behind the choices. It is technical precision with no soul.

If Cathy Corison tried to game her bottles using a data-crunching algorithm in the Enologix system, she might optimize a single year for a better wine score. But it would be at the cost of a much more compelling—and impressive— trajectory. "One of the things I love about wine is that it speaks of time and place, and marches forward speaking of time and place. These wines are still talking about what was happening," Corison told me. "I feel a moral obligation to make wines that let the dirt speak."

By making such wines for thirty years, Corison's vintages have remained remarkably consistent over the years. She doesn't add acid, tannins, enzymes, or any of the oak flavors. The wine that was dying to get out of her was based entirely on the grapes themselves. When you drink Cathy Corison's wine, you are experiencing everything she cares about: a profundity of data that can never be captured in an algorithm. Machine learning can never understand how she prevailed despite falling in and then out of style. And entering all the sense data possible wouldn't get at the meaning of her perseverance. Computers simply do not give a damn; they will never understand that caring is the whole point.

Meaningful Differences

Great philosophers like Martin Heidegger, Albert Borgmann, and Hubert Dreyfus argue that the kind of skill exhibited in the mastery displayed by Heen, Vestager, Voss, and Corison is the navigational skill of finding a perspective. At the heart of this navigation is a phenomenon they call *meaningful differences*.

To help understand this concept, first try to imagine a world *without* meaningful differences. This is the world of nihilism I described in corporate cultures that have lost their way. When we experience the world as lacking in meaningful differences, everything and everyone is merely a resource to be optimized. Resources are so fungible, they can be used to any end. Cathy Corison's grapes can be interchanged with steel from Margrethe Vestager's Italian factory. The extension of this understanding is that humans themselves are resources, hence the term *human resources*.

In perhaps his best essay, "The Question Concerning Technology," from 1954, Martin Heidegger describes this modern ideology, our world without meaningful differences. He cites technology as our modern way of "Being," our lens on the world. But his use of the word *technology* has very little to do with devices or other technical inventions. Technology—or technicity, as he calls it—is the logic that pervades our entire existence. Whereas Romans, or pre-modern societies, saw God's work in everything; and the Enlightenment thinkers felt that we humans were rulers of the universe, Heidegger argues that technology, today, is now at the center of our being. Not only has it replaced the gods, it has also replaced *us*.

In Heidegger's world, the spirit or logic of technology is "optimization": the relentless pursuit of squeezing every bit of value out of physical matter around us—including trees, water, and even people. Two hundred years ago, a carpenter would look at a piece of wood and work with it to make the finest creation possible—a door handle, say—given the grain and texture of that particular piece of wood. Today, however, we optimize wood by making all wood into wood pulp and reassembling it again as standardized, non-unique, and perfectly flexible "wood." In Heidegger's mind, this is the invisible structure that is ordering the reality of our world today: we standardize, optimize, and make things available and flexible.

In a Silicon Valley state of mind, we experience the malaise that Heidegger characterizes across all aspects of our daily lives. Everything is available; everything is equivalent to everything else: every day, hour, and second are the same as every other day, hour, and second. We are no different from all the other cogs and widgets being shipped here and there in the transportation system. Our school system is built to create flexible accountants that are interchangeable and available for use and optimization. Companies and governments can take in new people or throw them out again with great ease because everyone is trained in the same methods by the same institutions. Technology is what makes our existence so flexible, but it is also what makes it so easy to manipulate and then to dispose of. This is progress. Or is it?

Masters like Heen, Vestager, Voss, and Corison have a very special role to play in this age of technology. Their acts of phronesis—engaging in their worlds with a knowledge and experience that is necessarily context-dependent—work to dispel the modern malaise. They are not fungible resources in the global system of goods. Instead, they respond to the call of their worlds.

Hubert Dreyfus, professor of philosophy at the University of California, Berkeley, further explained the unique role of these kinds of masters to me: "When we finally understand mastery and this calling of the world, then we understand that the source of meaning in our lives isn't in us, as the Cartesian model suggests—it is in being in the world. When people are doing a skillful thing in the world, they lose themselves. The distinction between the master and the world disappears. Seeing what masters can do, and what we can do, we can all bring out what is best in ourselves."

With their craft, these masters give us a glimpse of what it is to transcend ourselves. But this type of journey takes courage. "Risk is absolutely important in acquiring any skills," Dreyfus told me, "because you have to leave the rules behind and leave behind what one generally does and stretch out into your own experience of the world. What distinguishes between risks we're interested in and mere bravado is whether the risks are taken in the interest of what one is committed to, what one has defined themselves in terms of, and what makes the meaningful differences in their life. That kind of a risk is a necessary step in becoming a master at anything."

In other words, you will never see meaningful differences unless you actually give a damn. Do you?

Chapter Eight

What Are People For?

All good things…come by grace and grace comes by art and art does not come easy.

—*Norman Maclean,* A River Runs Through It

I would try to make lists. A list of all the stores and businesses going up and down the main street and who owned them, a list of family names, names on the tombstones in the cemetery and any inscriptions underneath.…The hope of accuracy we bring to such tasks is crazy, heartbreaking. And no list could ever hold what I wanted, for what I wanted was every last thing, every layer of speech and thought, stroke of light on bark or walls, every smell, pothole, pain, crack, delusion, held still and held together—radiant, everlasting.

—*Alice Munro,* Lives of Girls and Women

The Future of Caring

A leading global provider of health care equipment and systems was trying to understand the future of long-term care for the elderly, especially given the aging populations in countries as varied as Japan, France, Canada, and the United States. We partnered with them for a sensemaking study that involved interviews and observations with more than 450 people across thirty-three different institutions in these four countries. The study included retirement homes, dementia homes, day care, and assisted living, and the goal was to form a perspective on where long-term care was headed and how the patient and caregiver experience was changing.

Until recently, the model for long-term care was following the curve of so many other rapidly growing industries. Financial pressures and the increasing elderly burden were—and still are—creating a strong demand for efficiency. Caregivers and their institutions felt a need to put more focus on the parts of the care that were easily measured and that provided an obvious return on investment—including a high resident-to-caregiver ratio, a low number of falls, and low occurrence of pressure ulcers. In this way, caregivers and institutions started to view the residents primarily through their bodily needs—bathing, toileting, moving in and out of bed—and they standardized their care to be as efficient as possible. As one caregiver in the study put it, "I don't want to say we are robots, but we do have a job to do . . . there simply isn't time getting to know them. You don't know their history."

This drive for efficiency in long-term care resembles the trajectory we know so well from the corporate farming system and its reliance on monoculture, or the education system and its drive for metrics, accountability, and standardized testing. This is the culmination of our modern era of management science: a highly optimized system that measures patients by quantitative accounts.

But a pattern emerged in the study that provides a new vision for long-term care. It is a development that has much to teach us about our attitudes toward abstracted knowledge in the form of measurements and returns on investment. Ultimately, it offers us a clearer understanding of what people are *for*.

Randall and the 3PM Solution

It is the changing of the shift at an assisted living facility in California, and "Randall," an 87-year-old resident, is beginning to grow agitated. This is a regular pattern with Randall, who suffers from dementia. The shift change—which occurs at 3 PM every day—is filled with the commotion of moving bodies, new faces, the whirl of change. It triggers something from deep inside Randall and he often starts acting out, engaging in angry conversations with his own hallucinations.

"Barbara," one of his caregivers, ushers Randall into the dining room and slowly, methodically, clears the rest of the residents out of the space. Randall starts to wander through the room, tipping tables and moving chairs. He grabs Barbara's arm and grips it with intensity for several seconds. She moves her arm away with a nonchalant comment, "I don't bend that way, dear." And then she tries to distract him: "Look at the light coming in the windows, Randall. Look at how bright it is out there." All the while she performs a subtle dance with the other residents. She gives some of them a tap, waking them up if they have fallen asleep at the table, offering them support while they get out of chairs and get out of the room. She glides seamlessly around residents in wheelchairs and walkers, pushing them one by one into the hallway so Randall can be isolated. When the room is completely empty except for Randall, she shuts the doors and stays to observe him, making certain he is safe by watching through the glass.

"We put him in the dining room so he can get his energy out," she told researchers in the study. "This space has more room for him and better light when he is feeling agitated. When the other residents see Randall in there, they know they don't want to be a part of it."

This type of distress is typical for residents with dementia, and it is a game changer in the world of long-term care. The Organisation for Economic Co-operation and Development (OECD) projects that between 2015 and 2035, dementia in the United States will increase by 55.6 percent. In Canada, they estimate an increase of 63 percent, and in Japan an increase of 74 percent. The agitation that typifies some dementia patients is so time-consuming for everyone involved that the entire model of efficient care is being turned upside down. Facilities need to focus on how to keep the mood of agitation from spreading and on how to minimize friction, both inside and outside of care tasks. Easily quantified measurements like occurrence of pressure ulcers have no bearing on the care a resident like Randall needs. What matters much more are the personalized strategies—artful hacks—that his caregivers perform every day.

This kind of care requires that the team of caregivers get to know Randall better, both his previous life and how he experiences being in the institution. For example, Barbara discovered that he was a schoolteacher for several decades. His reaction to the 3 PM shift change was not random. His muscle memory responded to the hours of the school day—the energy of the 3 PM release, with kids in the hallways and movement away from the classroom and toward home. When the shift change occurs at the facility, Randall feels confused and frustrated that he doesn't recognize his surroundings. He senses that something is going on but doesn't know what he is supposed to do. His caregiver team put these pieces together by placing his behavior in a context with his life outside the institution. Barbara calmed Randall down by addressing him as "Mr. Johnson," the name his students used in class. In anticipation of the chaos of 3 PM, she and the rest of the staff began distracting him with songs and stories while the new caregivers signed in.

"We've got it down to a kind of science," Barbara told the researchers. "Sometimes he just needs a change so we know when to switch people. Sometimes he responds really well to a softer voice that is almost like a whisper. But sometimes he needs you to respond in exactly the same tone as his. Almost like an echo of his voice. You kind of have to feel him out."

And when none of the artful hacks manage to calm him, Randall's team has devised a protocol. They guide him gently into the dining hall and isolate him briefly so he can "get his energy out."

Randall's caregiving strategies are written up on whiteboards and on typed sheets of paper and passed back and forth among his caregiving team: "Randall was a woodworker. Offer him Montessori blocks," and "Randall was a guidance counselor. Ask him about his work." There is no way to codify this type of knowledge, because it is only relevant for the care of one person: Randall. If his institution attempted to apply management science to it—to "scale up" this knowledge—they would find it difficult to apply. The best care involves getting to know each patient within a social context and then devising a series of strategies that best suit their individual needs.

This personalized caregiving may seem like an elaborate and costly strategy, but, in fact, Randall's facility has found that it is the most efficient way to deal with Randall and his dementia. With the right combination of hacks, cues, and distractions, they can get Randall bathed, fed, and calmed much faster than if they expediently checked off their list of bodily needs and ignored Randall's growing discomfort and specific triggers. And, it goes without saying, personalized caregiving aligns more fully with the vision of the caregivers. There is less burnout and stress and a greater sense of purpose for the staff when they are encouraged to get to know each patient as a person.

You might look at these examples and say, well, sure, we all want good care, but it's too expensive to maintain. What we are discovering, however, is that the real expense is care meted out only through management science and codified knowledge. As it turns out, good-quality personalized care is *cheaper* care when it comes to dementia. The cost-effectiveness is a direct result of its efficiency. According to caregivers and their management in every country we studied, this more personalized care of dementia patients saves time in the day. When the entire culture inside the facility is calmer and more peaceful—when friction is averted—fewer patients suffer from falls and there are fewer pressure ulcers. The entire system works better.

"The focus is shifting more from the task to the person," one administrator in the study told us. "If you can create relationships with the people you're caring for, it's going to be better for them. They're probably going to have fewer behaviors, more quality of life and peace. This then makes our work easier and quicker."

Such a shift necessitates a fundamental change in our assumptions about time and cost. This "new efficiency" in dementia care is entirely local and contextualized: it cannot be abstracted and scaled. Because there is no other Randall in the world, there is no standardized solution that can account for the behavior of Randall. Caregivers today rely on analog, "homemade" ways of sharing resident-specific knowledge— tips and tricks—with each other to make their work easier: notes on paper or whiteboards, or simply conversation. More can be done to make their experience-based, resident-specific knowledge readily available to them when it matters the most, often in care situations where residents easily become scared or agitated. The exciting potential of new technology is not that it makes standardized procedures quicker but that it can help support personalized care. In other words, caregivers need support knowing exactly which "buttons to push" with each resident and adapting the care accordingly—rather than support pushing the same buttons more and more quickly.

In many situations—certainly not all, but many—human intelligence is still the most efficient intelligence for addressing contextual challenges. It is an efficiency based not on scalable knowledge but on a profound understanding of the particular.

Breaking the Spell

At age 82, Wendell Berry is an American treasure. He has been farming the same plot of land in Henry County, Kentucky, for several decades as well as teaching at his alma mater, the University of Kentucky, and has written over forty works of fiction, nonfiction, and poetry. In the 1980s, from his porch on his farm, Berry had a front-row seat to the transforming landscape of American agriculture. He wrote a prescient essay in 1985 entitled, "What Are People For?" that serves as a perfect coda to our sensemaking journey.

In the essay, Berry tracks the development of increasing urbanization and the hollowing out of American rural life and community. He calls attention to the name economists give to the masses of people that used to work in the farmlands: the "permanently unemployable." According to the agricultural economists, these were the least efficient producers: "[T]oday, with hundreds of farm families losing their farms every day, the economists are still saying, as they have said all along, that these people deserve to fail...and the rest of us are better off for their failure."

The knowledge these people held and the work that they did has now been eradicated by varying combinations of machinery and chemicals. Some called this displacement a triumph of agricultural science, but Berry wonders what is going to happen to all those people now deemed useless. "Is the obsolescence of human beings now our social goal?" he asks.

Back in the 1980s, Berry's question referred primarily to the work and knowledge of the farm. But thirty-five years later we might say the same thing of almost every kind of human labor. Today it is white-collar jobs—accounting, radiology, law, journalism, and stock trading—that are endangered just as much as, if not more than, blue-collar jobs like farming, driving, and manufacturing. In 2013, Oxford University researchers argued that machines could perform almost half of U.S. jobs within the next twenty years.

These and other such statistics might prove to be inflated,

but there is no question that generalized IT systems and robotics play an important role in our lives today and in our futures. It is always worth celebrating developments that make our lives better and more meaningful, but what is to become of all the wisdom embedded in each and every one of these displaced jobs?

There is a vast wealth of knowledge contained in the small but significant gestures that occur in our worlds every single day. And we dismiss that knowledge at great risk to our future well-being, productivity, safety, and the nourishment of our own human spirits. When I echo Wendell Berry in asking "What are people for?," I am not suggesting that we do away with algorithms and machine learning. This is not a nostalgic call to return to the ways of the past, nor is it an attempt to hide away on a technology-free island. When I ask, "What are people for?," I am not asking an either/or question. Instead, I am reminding us that a culture frozen under a spell of the hard sciences is not much of a culture at all. When we revere technology and its solutions above all else, we stop seeing the agility and nuance that characterize human intelligence at its best. By putting technology above us, we stop synthesizing data from other sources. We miss out on a sustainable efficiency that comes from holistic thinking, not from optimization.

Most important for sensemaking, when I echo Wendell Berry's question, I ask why, in the Western world—and in America in particular—the idea of engaging in cultural inquiry has become a notion of needless luxury. Why are art, poetry, and music something we only dabble in as a hobby on weekends? Why is watching a play or going to a concert a privilege for snotty people, and reading a novel a waste of time? Art, we assume, is only relevant for the lucky few. "What's the impact to the bottom line?," people ask. There are no billable hours from time spent on stories or songs. Serious poetry and rigorous theory are discussed only by ladies who lunch. Snuggling up with a novel is my time, not productive time.

And yet, the answer to the question is clear: "What are people for?" *People are for making and interpreting meaning.* And the realm of the humanities is an ideal training ground for such an endeavor. It offers us more than two thousand years of material as our playground. Yes—of course—works in the humanities exist to bring us delight and pleasure. But they are also helpful, practical tools for dealing with the core questions of strategy that exist in any culture or organization: how to understand other worlds, customs, meanings, and competitive markets. These skills—at the heart of sensemaking—are the very skills that can never be outsourced. Machine learning will never come close to achieving insights into them. This is because they require a perspective, and algorithms simply have no point of view.

When you listen to Brahms, or try to understand the 1930s through the minimal but intensely soulful music of Son House, or sit down with the poetry of Sylvia Plath, you are also exercising analytical muscles that can make your start-up, your social enterprise, or simply your current position better. You can make it more fun and, above all else, more *truthful*. Let go of the shallow dogma of business schools and the promise of universal principles from the natural sciences. The humanities aren't a luxury; they are your competitive advantage.

So before you ridicule your daughter for wanting to study Confucian philosophy or look down on the people who choose to major in medieval French poetry, remember that you are quite likely working for such a person. It wouldn't be surprising if the chairman of the board or the president who runs your company is a former history major or really into Slavic studies or an expert on ancient Greek. If your son is truly passionate about math, by all means encourage him to go into the world of STEM. But pushing yourself or your children away from the humanities and into natural science solely as a utility function isn't actually very useful—either for them or for the future of our society. We certainly need masterful chemical engineers, mathematicians, and software developers, but we also need brilliant poets, singers, philosophers, and anthropologists. We need to synthesize the best ideas from all of these points of view, not attempt to optimize ourselves as individuals or as a culture.

For when we optimize ourselves, we lose sight of the meaningful differences between Randall—an old man with dementia—and any other old body taking up space in a residence. Optimization is about counting resources in an effort to scale them, and technology is the master of scale. But it need not be our master. Let us demote technology to a colleague or, better yet, a well-trained assistant or sidekick. When we claim our space as the sole interpreters of culture, we can emancipate ourselves and see technology for what it is: simply one more tool in the arsenal. It can help us to arrive at extraordinary places, but we still need to figure out what to do once we get there. The answers to that dilemma will only ever be solved by inspired acts of mastery that are drawn out of us by our context.

So when you go about your day today, I invite you to break the spell. Look around you. Listen for the moments when the pervasive mood of the culture is telling you to marvel at the magic of a new app that can track your digital footprints or a start-up in the health care space that can give you a real-time diagnosis for your symptoms. These are neat tricks—and useful ones at that. But we must remain more circumspect. Steve Jobs used to say, "This will change everything." Instead, try breaking the spell with this mantra: "This will change *some* things." After all, any broad-based education in the humanities shows us that nothing changes *everything*. Whether it is power dynamics, family strife, the rise and fall of great empires, our relationship to the gods, or our experience of falling in love, the ideas and stories and artistic works on offer in the humanities are always relevant. Our own human yearning for love, for knowledge, for purpose, and for excellence is never *new*, which is precisely why it never gets old.

Once the spell is broken, look around the world with fresh eyes. You might discover something extraordinary happening on our streets, in our homes, and at our schools every day. It is just as deserving of our wonder as the Hubble spacecraft or a Google-designed Go-playing algorithm. Today, if just for a moment, take some time to marvel at the way George Soros can experience knowledge about the market in his body. Or think about Bjarke Ingels, who allows contextual specificities—not conventions—to determine the shape of his buildings. Consider Sheila Heen, who is able to assess in a matter of seconds how a room filled with dozens of near strangers will best learn. Appreciate Margrethe Vestager and the ways she carves out space for human touchpoints within the hulking beasts of bureaucracy. Wonder at Chris Voss and his ability to decode shades of doubt, opportunity, manipulation, and anger within a message of negotiation. And make your best effort to taste the wine of Cathy Corison—for when you taste a Corison Cabernet, you are really tasting everything that Corison believes in. You are tasting one person's call to greatness within the context of a single plot of dirt.

Celebrate these and other masters of our world. And then look even closer. You will see magic of a more humble sort is all around us. You might see a schoolteacher create immediate cohesion and structure on the playground in a single gesture. Maybe you will bear witness to the work of a skilled manager taking the temperature of the team. It might be as simple as picking up a great novel from the past and entering—with full heart and head—into another world, connecting with another human across time and space.

There is so much to marvel at—from the most extraordinary heights of our greatest athletes, singers, politicians, and business leaders—right down to the mastery of a caregiver who knows to touch her patient's arm ever so gently.

"That noise must be the sound of your students in the hallway, Mr. Johnson." She says just the right thing at just the right moment in just the right way, and Randall is able to calm down and find peace at the end of the long day.

What are people for? Algorithms can do many things, but they will never actually give a damn. People are for caring.

Sources

Introduction: The Human Factor

The discussion around the decline of funding for the humanities was supported by a number of sources including: "The Heart of the Matter: The Humanities and Social Sciences for a Vibrant, Competitive, and Secure Nation," a 2013 bipartisan report put out by the American Academy of Arts and Sciences; "The Teaching of the Arts and Humanities at Harvard College: Mapping the Future," a study by Harvard University from 2013; and "Humanities Indicators: A Project of the American Academy of Arts and Sciences," last updated in October 2016.

I used the *Business Insider* article "30 People with 'Soft' College Majors Who Became Extremely Successful" from December 2012 to compile the list of leaders in finance, media, or policy with background in the humanities.

Chapter One: Making Sense of the World

The Alice Munro quote—"It's as if tendencies that seem most deeply rooted in our minds, most private and singular, have come in as spores on the prevailing wind, looking for any likely place to land, any welcome."—is from her story "Friend of My Youth," published in the *New Yorker* in 1990.

Chapter Three: Culture—Not Individuals

Nicole Pollentier's quotes are taken from several of our conversations in 2015 and 2016. The stanza from her poem "building pathways in the neuroplastic city" is included with her permission.

Chapter Four: Thick Data—Not Just Thin Data

The Story of the Three Traders: I pulled these narratives together from my conversations with Robert Johnson, Chris Canavan, and a handful of other traders who worked with George Soros at the Soros Fund. I also used quotes and ideas from George Soros's 1987 book *The Alchemy of Finance,* as well as reporting from the *Wall Street Journal* and the *New York Times.* Sebastian Mallaby's excellent 2010 book about hedge funds, *More Money Than God,* was an invaluable resource for some of the market details regarding "Black Wednesday" and "Black Monday."

Chapter Five: The Savannah—Not the Zoo

Husserl, Heidegger, and the Story of the Apricot Cocktail: Simone de Beauvoir describes this story in her 1962 memoir *The Prime of Life.* There is also a description of this encounter—as well as of Husserl's "phenomenological kindergarten" classes—in Sarah Bakewell's fascinating 2016 book *At the Existentialist Café: Freedom, Being, and Apricot Cocktails.*

Chapter Six: Creativity—Not Manufacturing

I took inspiration from Steven Watts's *The People's Tycoon: Henry Ford and the American Century* (2005) for the descriptions of Henry Ford's early days as an inventor and engineer at the opening of the chapter.

Robert I. Sutton's *Weird Ideas That Work: How to Build a Creative Company* (2001), and Chris Baréz-Brown's *How to Have Kick-Ass Ideas: Shake Up Your Business, Shake Up Your Life* (2008), are just two of countless examples of this type of "creative discourse" in business today.

Quotes on creativity:

The quotes from Saras D. Sarasvathy and Ben Baldwin are taken from a 2013 *Wall Street Journal* article entitled "How Entrepreneurs Come Up with Great Ideas."

The Mark Fields quote is from one of our conversations in 2015.

The Agatha Christie quote is from her 1977 autobiography: *Agatha Christie.*

George Soros's quote is from his book *The Alchemy of Finance* (1987).

The Tina Landau quote describing Phylicia Rashad is taken from the 2016 *New York Times* article: "Phylicia Rashad, Finding Joy in Tribulations of Her Role in 'Head of Passes.'"

Graham Green's *The End of the Affair* was published in 1951 and George Saunders's essay "The Braindead Megaphone" was published in 2007.

The Buddhist priest Zenkei Blanche Hartman's 2001

lecture on "Beginner's Mind" is available on the Chapel Hill Zen Center Website: www.chzc.org/hartman4.htm. Last accessed on November 8, 2016.

Flash of Insight: The Click:

The story of Bjarke Ingels and his quotes are taken from several of our conversations in 2015 and 2016.

Chapter Seven: The North Star—Not the GPS

I spent time with Sheila Heen, Margrethe Vestager, Chris Voss, and Cathy Corison in 2015 and 2016 and I used our conversations and reporting on their work to create these profiles of sensemaking at its most masterful.

Meaningful Differences:

These quotes from Hubert Dreyfus are taken from an interview I did with him at his office at the University of California, Berkeley, in May 2012.